Steady Hands Needed

Reflections on the role of the
Secretary of Foreign Affairs and Trade
in Australia 1979-1999

Steady Hands Needed

Reflections on the role of the
Secretary of Foreign Affairs and Trade
in Australia 1979-1999

edited by Trevor Wilson
and Graham Cooke

Published by ANU E Press
The Australian National University
Canberra ACT 0200, Australia
Email: anuepress@anu.edu.au
This title is also available online at: http://epress.anu.edu.au/steady_hands_citation.html

National Library of Australia
Cataloguing-in-Publication entry

Title:	Steady hands needed : reflections on the role of the Secretary of Foreign Affairs and Trade in Australia 1979-1999 / editors Trevor Wilson, Graham Cooke.
ISBN:	9781921536120 (pbk.)
	9781921536137 (pdf.)
Series:	ANZSOG series
Notes:	Bibliography.
Subjects:	Australia. Dept. of Foreign Affairs.
	Australia. Dept. of Foreign Affairs and Trade
	Australia--Foreign relations--1976-
	Australia--Foreign relations administration.
Other Authors/Contributors:	
	Wilson, Trevor
	Cooke, Graham.
Dewey Number:	327.94

All rights reserved. No part of this publication may be reproduced, stored in a retrieval system or transmitted in any form or by any means, electronic, mechanical, photocopying or otherwise, without the prior permission of the publisher.

Cover design by John Butcher.

Funding for this monograph series has been provided by the Australia and New Zealand School of Government Research Program.

This edition © 2008 ANU E Press

John Wanna, *Series Editor*

Professor John Wanna is the Sir John Bunting Chair of Public Administration at the Research School of Social Sciences at The Australian National University. He is the director of research for the Australian and New Zealand School of Government (ANZSOG). He is also a joint appointment with the Department of Politics and Public Policy at Griffith University and a principal researcher with two research centres: the Governance and Public Policy Research Centre and the nationally-funded Key Centre in Ethics, Law, Justice and Governance at Griffith University. Professor Wanna has produced around 17 books including two national text books on policy and public management. He has produced a number of research-based studies on budgeting and financial management including: *Budgetary Management and Control* (1990); *Managing Public Expenditure* (2000), *From Accounting to Accountability* (2001) and, most recently, *Controlling Public Expenditure* (2003). He has just completed a study of state level leadership covering all the state and territory leaders — entitled *Yes Premier: Labor leadership in Australia's states and territories* — and has edited a book on Westminster Legacies in Asia and the Pacific — *Westminster Legacies: Democracy and responsible government in Asia and the Pacific*. He was a chief investigator in a major Australian Research Council funded study of the Future of Governance in Australia (1999-2001) involving Griffith and the ANU. His research interests include Australian and comparative politics, public expenditure and budgeting, and government-business relations. He also writes on Australian politics in newspapers such as *The Australian*, *Courier-Mail* and *The Canberra Times* and has been a regular state political commentator on ABC radio and TV.

Table of Contents

About the editors	ix
Acknowledgements	xi
Foreword	xiii
Prologue: Steady hands needed for turbulent times – the DFAT secretaries 1979–99	1
Peter Henderson, AC	13
Stuart Harris, AO	27
Richard Woolcott, AC	39
Michael Costello, AO	53
Philip Flood, AO	67
Epilogue: 'The job is never done'	83
Appendix 1: Data on DFAT staff numbers and budget allocations	95

About the editors

Trevor Wilson was an Australian diplomat/civil servant for 37 years and is now retired and a Visiting Fellow on Burma at the ANU in Canberra. He was a member of the Australian International Affairs Canberra Branch Council in 2004–06

Graham Cooke has been a journalist for 44 years, having worked in Britain, New Zealand and Australia, the last 28 years in Canberra. He was a member of the Australian International Affairs Canberra Branch Council from 2004 to the present.

Acknowledgements

The editors are grateful for ANZSOG's support for this initiative and to Professor John Wanna and John Butcher for their help in preparing the manuscript for publication. We also wish to thank the Australian Institute of International Affairs Canberra Branch for their efforts in organising this project on the role of secretaries of the Department of Foreign Affairs and Trade in managing Australia foreign policy, particularly at a period of considerable change in Australia and in the world. We are most grateful to John Nethercote for his generous guidance and assistance in the preparation of this manuscript and to a former DFAT colleague for comments and suggestions on the prologue. The editors would also like to acknowledge the strong and unflagging support for this project from AIIA Canberra Branch Presidents Peter Hendy and Ian Dudgeon, as well as AIIA National CEO Melissa Conley-Tyler.

Foreword

The Australian Institute of International Affairs (AIIA) is an independent, non-profit organisation seeking to promote interest in and understanding of international affairs in Australia. The AIIA was formed in 1924, established as a federal body in 1933, and is the only nation-wide organisation of its kind in Australia. It is financed by members' contributions, a small government subvention, and tax-deductible donations from individuals and businesses. The Institute provides a forum for discussion and debate but does not seek to formulate or promote its own institutional views. It arranges programs of lectures, seminars, conferences and other discussions, and sponsors research and publications.

In 2006, the Council of the Canberra Branch of the AIIA initiated a lecture series of former secretaries of the Australian Department of Foreign Affairs and Trade. The Canberra branch benefited from the fact that a number of the former secretaries had remained resident in Canberra and continued to be members of the AIIA. It was thought that this was too good an opportunity to miss and so the lecture series was formulated.

In the end we have been very fortunate to obtain the participation of five of the eight living former secretaries. Over the period May to November 2006, Mr Peter Henderson AC, Mr Richard Woolcott AC, Dr Stuart Harris AO, Mr Philip Flood AO and Mr Michael Costello AO made presentations to members of AIIA at the national headquarters, Stephen House, Canberra.

We at the AIIA believe that the lecture series has been a particularly valuable contribution to the history of the administration of the foreign policy in Australia during the last 28 years, since the time Mr Henderson was appointed secretary of the then Department of Foreign Affairs in 1979. Never before have the experiences of so many former secretaries of Foreign Affairs, and its successor Foreign Affairs and Trade, been brought together in this way. Sadly, one secretary who served in this period, Dr Peter Wilsenski, died in 1994 after ill health cut short his term as secretary from 1992–93. We were also unable to schedule Dr Ashton Calvert, secretary from 1998–2006, before his tragic death in 2007.

The series covers the watershed amalgamation of the Department of Foreign affairs with the Department of Trade in 1987. A number of the speakers also provided some fascinating insights into major foreign policy issues that occurred over this momentous period in world history, which included the end of the Cold War, continuing problems in the Middle East, developments in Indonesia and the South Pacific and the rise of China.

The former secretaries have graciously agreed to have their speeches recorded in this volume and we extend our thanks to them for that. I would particularly like to congratulate Mr Trevor Wilson and Council Vice President Mr Graham Cook, who together shouldered the major burden in organising the events and who have now edited this volume. I would also like to thank the national office of the AIIA for the financial support in producing the publication.

Ian Dudgeon
President AIIA Canberra Branch
& member of the AIIA National Executive

Prologue: Steady hands needed for turbulent times – the DFAT secretaries 1979–99

Trevor Wilson

Foreign ministries the world over have many similar features, but they all differ significantly in their operational and staffing needs from their domestic ministry counterparts. Their essential work is the management of all aspects of bilateral relations between countries; they are also deeply involved in the activities of multilateral organisations and are routinely called upon to respond to unpredictable international events over which they have little or no control. At the high policy level, the subject matter of their work ranges from trade and security to human rights and the environment. For most of these pursuits, foreign ministries function according to international rules that are often also the subject of domestic laws to enforce them. At the other end of their responsibilities are the travel-related consular and passport services so much in demand in this age of globalisation. In this period, international events assumed much greater immediacy for domestic policy-makers, thanks mainly to the enormous improvements in communications which brought international events into the home more than ever before. For a variety of reasons, therefore, those running diplomacy need to be keenly aware of both the international environment in which they operate as well as domestic circumstances and implications. Presiding over the institution that manages a country's international relations on a daily basis is, therefore, no small task.

As an earlier review of the challenges for reforming Australia's foreign service acknowledged,[1] operationally, striking a balance between these sometimes competing interests requires particular judgment and finesse on a day-to-day basis. Ensuring that administrative systems, communications infrastructure and personnel practices (recruiting, training, postings) meet the needs of such a diverse and unpredictable agenda calls for longer-term vision, steadiness of direction and commitment to outcomes. Also, educating and informing other affected parties, whether at home or abroad, is critically important. Instant communications has meant more, not less, pressure on the system, its employees and, above all, its managers. In many respects, higher levels of probity, a greater degree of accountability and much more transparency have come to be the hallmark of most Australian government agencies and Australia's foreign service has not been exempt from this trend.

The position of secretary of the Australian Department of Foreign Affairs and Trade (DFAT) is a senior position in the Australian Public Service. With a staff (including overseas staff) numbering around 3,500 in 2007, it is a middle-sized department (for comparison, the Department of Agriculture, Fisheries and Forestry has 4,200, while Treasury only has 921). Appendix 1 summarises the changes in staff numbers and the breakdown in types of staff over this period. The number of Australia-based staff which initially declined, subsequently increased as security concerns developed world-wide, but the number of locally engaged staff — critical for the operations of overseas missions — declined by around 25 per cent as part of ongoing budgetary constraints. Despite its increasingly well-known responsibilities for passports and consular services, DFAT is not primarily a 'client service' department with the special demands that these departments make of staff. Nevertheless, being secretary of this department — with its multi-faceted operations, demanding time-sensitive response requirements and its manifestation of complex and sometimes contradictory national interests — is by any measure a challenging job.

If anything, the extent of change that occurred within DFAT during the period 1979–99 is somewhat understated in the following chapters. In 1979, the Department of Foreign Affairs was not very different from what it had always been: an organisation with a strong distinctive view of itself as being rather different from the rest of the Australian Public Service (APS) in its commitment to a 'higher' plane of international relations based on commonly accepted and inviolable rules and procedures.

Then, in 1987, as part of an industrial agreement, the long-established specialised 'streams' among DFAT staff (diplomatic versus consular and administrative staff) were notionally abolished. Within the department, the designation of DFAT officers as 'Foreign Affairs Officers' was abandoned as DFAT personnel were fully integrated into the APS, sharing the same administrative designations and working conditions as the rest of the APS. Moreover, given DFAT's reputation for being hierarchical, with discriminatory internal career paths, it only adjusted with difficulty to the public service reforms introduced by the Hawke Labor Government from 1983 that called for greater delegation of decision-making, more openness and greater fairness in working conditions and recruitment throughout the service. Initially, DFAT had grown considerably from the 1970s, taking on new responsibilities against a background of significant cultural change in the public sector, but by 2000 its numbers had reduced to 8 per cent below the level of 1980. While in absolute terms its budget had trebled, its outlays fell as a proportion of government outlays from 1.99 per cent to 1.22 per cent (see Appendix 1).

Specifically, the decade 1982–92 was a period of intense and relentless public stress for DFAT management, in which successive secretaries were deeply involved. A series of 'whistleblower' allegations of corruption, mismanagement and poor morale prompted a major inquiry by the Senate Standing Committee on Finance and Public Administration.[2] At the time, departmental leadership was absorbed in repeated efforts to exorcise these demons that, on the one hand, often smeared their personal reputations and, on the other, cast a damaging pall over the department's personnel management. The passage of time seems to have dulled the memory of how trying these events were for particular DFAT secretaries. In the words of the Senate Committee: 'the cultural change in DFAT (from reliance on personal relationships to the use of more formal management systems) … must have added considerably to the stress experienced by many officers and the Department as a whole.'

While the findings of the Senate Committee inquiry essentially vindicated the leadership of the Department, which had done 'as well as could be expected,' the Committee noted that:

> DFAT did not manage aspects of the process of change in a satisfactory manner … However, it is clear that the changes have been large and rapid and DFAT must be given credit for the progress it has made (Senate 1992: 155).

Essentially, the inquiry found some signs of 'systemic management failure' but said the department had generally performed satisfactorily and insisted that its criticisms 'did not go to any major aspect of the Department's management and operations' (Senate 1992:156). It did, however, call for renewed efforts by DFAT management to achieve better levels of accountability, transparency and fairness, and identified 37 'housekeeping areas' where it recommended improvements be made. However, a minority report submitted by Liberal Party members of the committee questioned whether DFAT had really resolved many of the issues satisfactorily and sought further evidence that it was in fact managing its operations effectively.

One of the underlying challenges for DFAT secretaries then, and ever since, was the extent to which the department needed specialised staff in areas such as trade policy, public information, international law, economics and country experts. While successive secretaries argued the case for the greater flexibility that multi-skilling delivered, in later years the value of retaining substantial specialist expertise came to be recognised. 'Specialist' skills included language skills which the department traditionally fostered in Australian diplomats, yet the only former language officer to become secretary of the department was Dr Ashton Calvert, who was appointed in 1998. In sum, no secretary of DFAT could ignore the need for staff who were able to operate effectively and in Australia's interests at the intersection of cultures.

By any measure, the changes to the organisational culture and structure of DFAT between 1980 and 2000 were dramatic. Some of these changes were those that occurred within the APS as a whole, such as performance management and performance pay, but there were additional changes — internal and external — that affected Foreign Affairs specifically. By 1999, for example, DFAT staff were promoted and remunerated in the same way as their peers in other departments; any distinctive 'foreign service' features had gone. Symbolic of this enormous shift, their separate and strongly representative staff association (which had always dealt with management alongside the traditional unions) had been disbanded, to be replaced, eventually, by a loosely organised association with a small membership, no formal industrial negotiating role and little profile.[3] By the early 1990s, DFAT SES members were, like their counterparts in all other departments, employed on Australian Workplace Agreements (which were individually signed but collectively negotiated agreements) while the remainder of the staff were on a collectively negotiated Certified Agreement, in line with the practice in other APS departments, which was a significant change.

Without a doubt the most significant event affecting departmental culture was the promulgation in 1987 of changed Administrative Arrangements that brought 490 new staff with different backgrounds and responsibilities into the department from the former Department of Trade and from the Australian Information Service.[4] It was no small shock for staff to find themselves working closely alongside public servants from different backgrounds who, at first, even used a different computer network, and considerable departmental leadership was required for some period to communicate loudly, clearly and consistently that a new approach to their work was expected. Organisationally, many staff found themselves in the same work unit as people hailing from another organisation, although some more technical trade negotiators, for example, remained in much the same structure as before. These differing approaches were deliberate, as it was felt that all staff had to be challenged to pursue more sophisticated policy-making while valuable technical skills (in multilateral trade negotiation, for example) should not be lost. The secretaries concerned took both a cautious yet radical line to ensure that more integrated policy formulation occurred. Interestingly, most staff responded extremely well and surprised the departmental executive by requesting a deeper integration of staff within a few months. Before long, many staff sought to cross over into new work.

This major reorganisation was not a 'world first'. In 1983, Canada had created a Department of Foreign Affairs and International Trade.[5] More cooperative, complex policies better attuned to the needs of the times were soon to emerge from Canberra as well and, in time, it was also realised that leaving the Australian Trade Commission and the Export Finance Insurance Corporation initially in other portfolios was an incomplete arrangement. Yet the Australian experiment was quickly deemed successful, was eventually recognised as something that should not be reversed, and went on to be copied by several other countries. For the DFAT secretary, one of the challenging aspects of the amalgamated department was the parallel requirement for the secretary to serve two ministers who would not always enjoy entirely harmonious relationships nor always present departmental staff with fully sychronised tasking. In this dual role, DFAT secretaries are to this day called upon to exercise more than the usual amount of political discretion, mostly without problems ever becoming apparent.

The other area of major transforming change for Foreign Affairs, occurring roughly at the same time (1985–90), was in telecommunications technology. Telecommunications had always been a central feature of the department's operations which included formal responsibility for the government's overseas communications. All the secretaries contributing to this publication showed leadership and considerable readiness to take risks in adopting new communications technology that would significantly transform the nature of the department's daily operations. Reports and information that had previously taken time to reach the department were now available in real time and almost immediately. This transformed ministerial, management and public expectations of government reaction times and added to the burden on DFAT staff for immediate responses. It may have also contributed to the eventual shift away from medium-term policy planning. But DFAT's performance in this area of modern telecommunications, even though it did not meet all the targets set, was very credible in comparison with other foreign services. (As late as 2000, in some overseas posts DFAT telecommunications capabilities were ahead of the US State Department.)

Reviewing the recollections of the DFAT secretaries in this publication, however, one is also struck by what the DFAT secretary is and what they are not. In their authoritative *Making of Australian Foreign Policy*, Alan Gyngell and Michael Wesley comment on the considerable authority enjoyed by the DFAT secretary, but in fact give few examples of how this power might have been exercised. In fact, the DFAT secretary's authority in the period under consideration — from 1979 to 1998 — was considerably less than it might have been in the past. The main reason for this is the reassertion of ministerial control that accompanied the Hawke Government's 1983 reforms of the public service and administrative arrangements. Since then, there has been no doubt that the minister exercised the final authority and that even many administrative matters formally within the jurisdiction of the secretary, could not be decided by him without consultation with the minister.

The secretary of DFAT is more like a CEO of an organisation where many key decisions are made above him. Crucial in performing the job is giving operational direction and purpose to the organisation and its staff. This does not come from the minister or any other person. But the secretary of DFAT cannot be across all the detail of running the department. For example, the challenge of managing the financial accounting — with so many remote branches and in multiple currencies — is obviously great. It is not surprising that DFAT was one of the first departments to appoint a professional chief finance officer from outside the department.

Changes in the *Public Service Act* in 1976 had also affected the manner in which secretaries of departments were appointed. These replaced a simple procedure for appointment by the Governor-General with a selection committee conducted by the Chairman of the Public Service Board (PSB) to advise the Prime Minister so that he could make a recommendation to the Governor-General. Peter Henderson was among the first to be appointed under this new procedure. When Henderson was replaced by Stuart Harris in 1984, a greatly streamlined process required the Prime Minister to receive a report from the Chairman of the PSB which would be the basis for a recommendation to the Governor-General. Following the abolition of the PSB in 1987, this advisory role was transferred to the secretary of the Department of the Prime Minister and Cabinet. By the time of the 1999 amendment of the *Public Service Act*, the appointment of secretaries had become the responsibility of the Prime Minister himself, not the Governor-General. In this period as well, governments assumed greater latitude in setting the remuneration and other employment conditions of departmental heads, with the Remuneration Tribunal's role shifting from one of determination to advice. One result was a greater mix in the remuneration package between salary and other items, with superannuation allocations becoming increasingly popular.

Until the 1970s, there was no formal provision or standard practice for the termination of the appointment of a departmental secretary. Before that, the principal means of replacing an 'unwanted' departmental head was the device of abolishing the whole department. However, the 1984 changes included a removal process and were accompanied by a new policy that appointments would be reviewed at five-yearly intervals. The new arrangements included provision for compensation in the event of early termination. By the 1990s, significant performance pay provisions for departmental secretaries had been introduced. The consequence of all these changes is that, today, the secretary of DFAT along with his counterparts in the APS can be removed much more readily than in the past. The position, however, is much more generously remunerated, although certainly not on the scale of CEOs of business organisations of a comparable size and with a comparable budget to manage.

Parallel with these changes were the obligations that secretaries assumed under the new *Financial Administration Act* of 1997 that reinforced their long-standing responsibilities for managing their department's finances. Secretaries assumed additional financial responsibilities from those previously carried out by the

Treasury and, later, the Department of Finance or the Public Service Board (before its abolition). However, secretaries also enjoyed considerable latitude in how they carried out their responsibilities. Although there was considerable devolution of responsibility, the corollary of this was potentially more searching accountability. One result was a much greater level of parliamentary scrutiny of departmental administration following growth of the Senate Committee system since 1970 and the House of Representatives committee system established in 1987. Hand in hand with these changes was a broader remit for the Auditor-General, under new audit legislation.

Most of the expansion of the management role of departmental secretaries occurred in the period covered by this publication. This represented a transformation of the position, without in any way diminishing the secretary's obligations for providing advice on policy and overseeing the formulation of that advice. As a result, the modern secretary has more diverse responsibilities, considerable latitude in the way departmental staff are organised, as well as a wider range of relationships outside the department. Above all, secretaries have a higher requirement for accountability on all matters to their ministers.

Some matters always remained outside the secretary's control, such as the terms and conditions of employment determined by the Public Service Board (even if there was some discretion over salaries within the agreed budget). Employment conditions for departmental staff, whether overseas or in Australia, were the same as those that applied to staff from all departments. Some 'Heads of Mission' appointments were decided by the minister — or even the Prime Minister. The selection of deputy secretaries and first assistant secretaries, previously decided by selection processes within the department (subject to appeal), became the responsibility for selection panels including representatives from other departments, as is the case elsewhere in the public service.

Following the establishment of the Office of National Assessments (ONA) in 1977, moreover, DFAT was no longer the sole arbiter and judge of assessing political and economic developments in other countries, as they had been in the past. Significantly, ONA reports directly to the Prime Minister but DFAT only has input into, yet limited influence over, its assessments. Initially, ONA was staffed by many DFAT officers on secondment and has itself only ever been headed by former DFAT senior officers but, as time passed, many of the ex-DFAT staff did not return. A consequence of this was that ONA gradually built up its own, sometimes formidable, areas of expertise, which DFAT also once had but gradually, and perceptibly, lost. Moreover, DFAT's in-house analytical skills were also noticeably reduced as a long-term result of the assessment responsibility moving to ONA. Understandably, in these circumstances successive DFAT secretaries sought to re-emphasise DFAT's role in policy formulation, but this coincided with the appearance of new Australian policy implementers, such as the Department of Education, on Australia's international stage.

Similarly, as the public service was increasingly called on to respond to immediate issues of the day, as global communications became more 'instant', longer-term policy development that was in the 1960s and 1970s a matter of departmental pride, also suffered, to be officially abolished in the 1990s. Instead, the department found itself spending much larger proportion of its time and resources on consular matters, which became a topic of much greater media interest from the 1980s. This, along with the responsibility for passport issue (which DFAT had taken over from the Department of Immigration in 1974), transformed the department into much more of a service agency than an organisation focused largely on issues of high policy.

Little attention is given in the former secretaries' presentations to the challenges they faced in cutting staff, yet these were among the more difficult issues they faced throughout this period, especially as DFAT often seemed to have 'no friend in court' in cabinet (or the Expenditure Review Committee) when it came to defending the department's budget. So decisions to cut policy planning altogether or to expand consular and passport operations significantly were pragmatic decisions taken by secretaries reflecting the demands of the day, under never-ending resource pressures, and did not necessarily reflect ideal outcomes for secretaries with strong commitments to the department.

Over the years, the consistent appointment of DFAT secretaries from within the ranks of the department would have contributed emphatically to preservation of the departmental professionalism, if not its former culture (this is consistent with the practice in most other countries, where the concept of a distinct 'foreign service' is also much stronger). Only two complete outsiders have been appointed as secretary of DFAT: Stuart Harris, who had served previously as Deputy Secretary of Trade; and, in 2004, Michael L'Estrange, who had worked in the international division of the Department of the Prime Minister and Cabinet and was an outside appointee as High Commissioner to the UK. This contrasts markedly with other APS departments, where 'outside' appointments are much more common. Moreover, some senior DFAT officers have been appointed heads of other departments and agencies; this happened occasionally from the 1960s but more frequently from the mid-1990s,[6] but the reverse movement has not happened. It is curious that in the 20 years 1987–2007, there were only two ministers for Foreign Affairs while there have been seven secretaries of the department. Only one secretary in these two decades, Ashton Calvert, was appointed for a second term. Calvert was the only secretary of Foreign Affairs since Arthur Tange (1954–65) to serve for more than five years. Other than Tange, only Hodgson (1935–45) served for such a long term.

Traditionally, DFAT staff had been seconded to other departments (and sometimes the private sector, as in the case of Peter Henderson) and this broadened their experience, helped their networking and refreshed DFAT's own knowledge and expertise. As career mobility generally increased, secondments tended to disappear in the period from the mid-1980s. DFAT staff still moved to the Department of the Prime Minister and Cabinet and the Prime Minister's Office and vice versa. In this sense, DFAT became somewhat less 'isolated' than before, although in the late 1990s and thereafter this was partially compensated for by the increase in 'lateral recruitment'. However, even after the 1987 integration of trade staff into the department, there were no formal staff exchanges with Austrade and little or no mobility between the two organisations. Nor was there ever much movement between DFAT and AusAID, even though, arguably, development assistance expertise would be valuable in certain areas of DFAT policy implementation.

One phenomenon of the 1970s and 1980s was the increasing number of officers from other departments assigned to Australian missions overseas. While the former secretaries refer to formal mechanisms that DFAT traditionally employed and, indeed, refined, to manage the greater diversity of staff in overseas missions and coordinate the multiple lines of reporting, they do not really address the net result of more departments having an 'international branch' to which their own overseas staff reported. Yet the practice whereby other officials, when serving overseas, were formally seconded to DFAT, as is the case in many other countries, was still not widely enforced. Moreover, the presence of these representatives in Australia's overseas missions was not always problem-free. This change naturally complicated DFAT's policy role, made it more difficult for DFAT to keep track of the specialised and sometimes technical issues that arose. Overall, as a result, DFAT's voice in Australia's responses to some issues was diluted and generally its policy influence was eroded. So it is not altogether surprising that, during this period, the concept of the 'Australian foreign service' was neither advocated, nor was this terminology often used. Austrade (always under its own legislation) and some other departments would not necessarily recognise that they were part of an Australian foreign service. For example, the secretary of DFAT is not generally recognised, even informally, as the head of the Australian foreign service, whereas the secretary of the Department of the Prime Minister and Cabinet is often perceived and treated as the *de facto* head of the Australian Public Service.

While the DFAT institution is strong and the culture pervasive and enduring, many developments that occurred during this period contributed to a dilution of the departmental culture. Reinforcement of the departmental culture is achieved in part through training and early career instruction. But from the mid-1980s, DFAT stopped running its own training courses and outsourced these to Australian universities. Even though departmental staff still acted as 'lecturers', this meant a gradual dissipation of the departmental culture over time. Strangely, perhaps, there was never any joint training with Austrade or AusAID staff within the same portfolio, nor are there regular staff exchanges with either of those agencies (although staff transfers occasionally occur as one-off events). The 1992 Senate Committee report criticised the 'paternalistic management style' with its 'reliance on individual relationships'; the 'closed shop' limiting recruitment of 'outsiders' into the department; career prospects of officers already in the department; the lack of reinvigorating mobility between DFAT and other departments; and the 'insular' character of the department which discouraged talented people from joining. While it noted the significant improvements that had been made in most of these areas, it called on the department 'not to be complacent', to 'continue to make rigorous efforts to improve its administration' and to be 'continually alert to areas of potential regression or management failure' (Senate conclusions 13.9 1992).

All of the secretaries whose words appear in this publication made significant contributions to the department, but the nature of their contributions was obviously influenced by their individual qualities and experience, and by the circumstances in which they served. Some, such as Stuart Harris, had a greater impact as reformers than others, but this was not necessarily the result either of choice or natural leaning alone. Sometimes the secretaries were presented with a reform mandate, or found themselves in a situation where the department needed to keep pace with reform occurring in the public service around it. Some had a high public profile in their job, others less so.

The personal backgrounds of these secretaries were quite different, although their professional careers have some similarities. The two more 'traditional' diplomats, Peter Henderson and Richard Woolcott, both went to Geelong Grammar School, while Stuart Harris was born and attended high school in the UK. As bureaucrats, all experienced working closely with ministers and had been exposed to political processes. Significantly, four of the five had spent the formative years of their careers in Foreign Affairs, with a mixture of overseas and head office experience. But three (Harris, Flood and Costello) had experience of working in senior positions in other departments, while two (Henderson and Woolcott) had spent their entire working careers in DFAT. Richard Woolcott had spent more time overseas than his fellow secretaries. He had, however, spent some years as head of the Department's media office, giving him unusual breadth of knowledge about the workings of the department. For all the former secretaries, except Philip Flood, their bureaucratic careers ended with their term as secretary; Flood was subsequently appointed Australian High Commissioner to the UK.

By the year 2000, the department was demonstrably a more confident institution than the one of the 1980s. Talk of the department being 'in crisis' or suffering 'poor morale' had stopped as DFAT secretaries gave priority to ensuring departmental staff gave the governments of the day what they required. For example, DFAT had helped ensure that Australian interests remained secure in the later 1990s notwithstanding considerable turmoil in the Australian region (Fiji, East Timor, Papua New Guinea, Vanuatu and the Solomon Islands) where Australia for the first time could not depend on 'great and powerful allies'. The department had already produced Australia's first foreign policy white paper for the Howard government and was about to prepare a second version. Perhaps more than anything else, this was a revival of both the department's pre-eminent role in policy-making in international affairs and an affirmation of the role of the secretary in overseeing this process.

It is curious, however, that no history of the department has ever been written and that three of the former secretaries in this volume are among the relatively few senior DFAT officers who have ever written about the operations of the Department.

References

Beaumont, Joan et al. 2003, *Ministers, Mandarins and Diplomats: Australian Foreign Policy Making 1941-67*, Melbourne University Press.

Edwards, Peter 2006, *Arthur Tange: Last of the Mandarins*, Allen & Unwin, Sydney.

Gyngell, Alan and Michael Wesley 2003, *Making of Australian Foreign Policy*, Cambridge University Press, Cambridge.

Harris, Stuart 2002, 'The merger of the Foreign Affairs and Trade Departments revisited', *Australian Journal of International Affairs*, Volume 56, Issue 2 July 2002, pages 223-235. http://www.informaworld.com/smpp/title~content=t713404203~db=all~tab=issueslist~branches=56 - v5656,

Henderson, Peter 1986, *Privilege and Pleasure*, Methuen, North Ryde (NSW).

Henderson, Peter, 1987, 'Foreign Affairs and the Role of the Media', *Australian Journalism Review*, 9: 1&2, pp. 48-53:

Henderson, Peter, Stuart Harris and Richard Woolcott 2002, *Managing Australian Diplomacy: Three Views From the Top*, Australian Institute of International Affairs, Victorian Branch

Maley, William 2000, 'Australia and the East Timor Crisis: some critical comments' [online] Australian Journal of International Affairs, v.54, no.2, July: 151-161. Availability: <http://search.informit.com.au.virtual.anu.edu.au/fullText;dn=200100717;res=APAFT> ISSN: 1035-7718 [cited 31 Jan 08].

Senate Committee on Finance and Administration 1992, *Management and operation of the Department of Foreign Affairs and Trade*, Commonwealth of Australia, Canberra.

Verspaandonk, Rose 2003, 'Changes in the Australian Public Service 1975-2003', *Chronology No 1*, Parliamentary Library.

Woodard, Garry 2000, 'Ministers and mandarins: the relationships between ministers and secretaries of External Affairs 1935-1970' [online]. *Australian Journal of International Affairs*, v.54, no.1, Apr 2000: 79-95.

Woolcott, Richard 2003, *The Hot Seat: Reflections on Diplomacy from Stalin's Death to September 11*, Harper Collins Publishers, Melbourne.

ENDNOTES

[1] Anthony Milner and Trevor Wilson 1986 (eds), *Challenges and Options for the Department of Foreign Affairs*, Australian Institute of International Affairs Occasional Paper No 5, 1986.

[2] Entitled *Management and Operation of the Department of Foreign Affairs and Trade*, the report by the Senate Standing Committee on Finance and Public Administration was published in December 1992. This was two years after a performance audit of the Department by the Australian National Audit Office.

[3] Formal unions representing public servants or journalists across the public service had always been active in DFAT and its predecessors as well, but by the end of the 1990s had become the main voice for staff.

[4] In all, 350 trade officers and 140 Promotion Australia officers joined 2,300 Foreign Affairs officers (many of whom were local staff in Australia's overseas missions). Cited by Richard Woolcott in his contribution to *Managing Australia's Diplomacy: Three Views from the top*, AIIA (Victorian Branch) Occasional Paper No 2, 1989.

[5] In Canada, this involved 4,200 Canada-based staff and 3,600 overseas-based staff. See paper by Gordon Osbaldeston, former Under Secretary of External Affairs in *Australian Diplomacy: Challenges and Options for the Department of Foreign Affairs*, A.C. Milner and Trevor Wilson (eds) AIIA, 1989.

[6] Early heads of other departments include Sir Peter Heydon (Immigration), Sir David Hay (Territories), Sir Arthur Tange (Defence), Keith Shann (Public Service Board), Bill Pritchett (Defence) and Peter Wilenski (Labour, Education and Youth Affairs, Public Service Board, Transport and Communications). Later appointees include Chris Conybeare (Immigration), Sandy Hollway (Industry, Science and Technology, Employment, Education and Training), David Sadleir (Australian Security Intelligence Organisation), Joanna Hewitt (Agriculture), Bill Farmer (Immigration and Ethnic Affairs), Dennis Richardson (Australian Security Intelligence Organisation), and Ric Smith and Nick Warner (Defence).

Peter Henderson, AC

Secretary of the Department of Foreign Affairs, 1979–84

Background

The major international event over this period was the Soviet invasion of Afghanistan in 1979. Australian foreign policy was affected not only because of the debate over sanctions leading up to the 1980 Moscow Olympics, but also because of general concerns about expanding Soviet activities in Australia's nearby regions. In Asia, Vietnam's invasion of Cambodia in 1979 and the flow-on from China's 1978 'open door' policy represented different challenges and Australia had varying success as it adjusted its policies towards Japan (embarking on its 'resources diplomacy') and Indonesia (which was hyper-sensitive about internal stability).

Before taking up his appointment as secretary of the Department, Peter Henderson had a distinguished diplomatic career in Australia and overseas. But it was as a very experienced manager in the department that he had made his mark and he was always considered to be a prime candidate for the secretaryship. Writing about his appointment, one authoritative commentator noted that he 'brought to his task a capacity for hard work, considerable experience of in-house administration and a warm, sensitive, even democratic personality'.[1] These qualities were needed as the Department coped with internal morale problems, caused partly by budget cuts that affected it more than other departments, and increased challenges to its professionalism.

These years were also notable for the beginning of new dynamics affecting Australian foreign policy-making processes in Canberra. On the one hand, Prime Minister Malcolm Fraser continued to be an activist in the field of diplomacy, often demonstrating a distinctive and innovative approach, and the Office of National Assessments was set up to report directly to him which, to some extent, diminished the role of the Department of Foreign Affairs. Second, several outside reports on Australia's international relations had been commissioned by the Australian Government around this time implying some loss of confidence in traditional policy-making processes. These included the report on *Australia's Relations with the Third World*, by Professor Owen Harries (1980) and the *Report on Australia's Relations with Japan* by Baillieu Myer (1978). Thirdly, the Australian parliament displayed greater interest in Australia's international relationships, producing several reports from the Senate Foreign Affairs Committee (such as its 1980 report on Australia's Relations with ASEAN) whose recommendations tended to go beyond current government policies. Finally, after the *Freedom of Information Act* was enacted in 1982, Australian journalists were emboldened to write more critically about foreign policy. These were challenging times.

Peter Henderson published his 1986 autobiography *Privilege and Pleasure* (Methuen Haynes, 1986).

Henderson Presentation: 25 May 2006

I have been asked to speak about my role as secretary of the Department of Foreign Affairs. That was from 1979 to 1984, before the amalgamation with the Department of Trade. My talk focuses on what the job entailed and how I approached it, not on particular policy issues, or on Australia's external relationships, or on the political context of the day.[2]

One other thing before I go further. I must remind you it is now over 20 years — or two decades to use that fashionable and overworked word — since I was secretary. That is a very long time: a whole generation. I emphasise this for two reasons. My memory of the details of the events which took place over 20 years ago is now a bit porous. And if at times I sound somewhat out of date, I am.

A friend of mine has described the job like this:

- Responsible under the minister and cabinet for framing and implementation of foreign policy, bilateral and multilateral.
- Responsible for day-to-day management of a large institution with a mobile and diverse membership.

If that describes the job, how did I go about it? Let me begin with the ministerial and parliamentary, responsibilities. I shall go on later to the responsibilities of the day-to-day management of the department as an institution.

There are, I believe, two major determinants in the role that any departmental secretary plays in relation to the minister and the Government. First, there is the nature and personality of the secretary himself, shaped largely by his previous career experience and his general outlook and attitude of mind. Second, there is the minister of the day, *his* outlook and expectations. And overarching both, of course, is the key question of whether the minister and the secretary can develop a successful working relationship.

So how did I become secretary? And having been appointed, what did I actually do in the job? It is easy enough to answer the first question. It is very hard not to be long-winded in answering the second.

I became secretary because I was tapped on the shoulder for it. There was no application, no interview, no requirement to provide some sort of policy statement beforehand, no fixed term. My appointment, like others before it, came about as a result of consultation between the prime minister (Malcolm Fraser) and the minister (Andrew Peacock). Who else they consulted I simply do not know.[3]

In my case I had the advantage — at least I suppose it was an advantage — of being a known quantity to both of them: I had acted in the job for some seven months at different intervals over the preceding three years, first after Alan Renouf left and again after Nick Parkinson's departure.[4] It has been suggested to me that I was appointed because I was Sir Robert Menzies' son-in-law. I do not think the family relationship was a factor on this occasion.

I referred a moment ago to a public policy statement, or rather the lack of it. This did not mean that I had no idea of what I wanted to do as secretary. And what I wanted to do was in many respects the outcome of what I had seen and done in the department over the preceding 28 years. Careers were and, I suppose still are, very much governed by chance: what posts you are sent to, what jobs you are given in Canberra, how long you stay in any one assignment, health, family problems and so on.

In my case my general approach was influenced very heavily by the three-and-a-half years I had spent as a First Secretary in the personnel and administrative division of the department. Then, later on, I was First Assistant Secretary, Management Services and later again a deputy with some management and personnel responsibilities. I did not choose that career path. It just happened. Indeed, at one stage I was so depressed about the way I seemed to have been typecast that I applied for a transfer to the Defence Department. But I was much cheered to come back from London in 1970 and to be put in charge of the South and South East Asia Branch. I found it much more enlivening and more of a challenge, to be drafting a message from Mr Whitlam to Washington about Vietnam, than yet another long statement for the secretary to be sent to a promotions appeal committee at the Public Service Board.

Naturally, and this must be true of anyone appointed secretary from within the Department, I was also very much influenced by my perceptions of how my predecessors had handled the job. I had worked closely with some of them. There were, to my mind, a number of lessons to be drawn — examples to be followed, examples *not* to be followed. For example, I had seen at first hand the benefits to individual officers if the secretary took a painstaking approach to individual career aspirations and problems, and to be accessible to staff. I had also seen what happened if the paper was not kept moving and filing cabinets were stuffed higgledy-piggledy with files needing decisions. I had also noted the consequences of the secretary making no real effort to work with, or for the Department to be accepted by, the rest of the Commonwealth public service.

High on the lists of the fields of activity where one tried to learn from observing the behaviour of one's predecessors was the question of the relationship to be established with the minister. The record was, on the whole, a daunting one. There were a number of known, or suspected, cases of extreme difficulty. Senior officers had for years given us spine-chilling accounts of confrontations with Dr Evatt,[5] but he was not the only one. In some instances we had to wait for many years to know what actually happened. One recent example is Peter Edwards' account in his book published only a few months ago of Sir Arthur Tange's treatment by Sir Paul Hasluck.[6]

The actual circumstances varied in every case, depending on the pressure of events at the time and on individual personalities. There is no golden mean that I know of, no commonly accepted way, for a minister and a secretary to proceed. It is a testing relationship which has to be worked out from scratch each time by two often very different people.

Looking at the issue from the point of view of the secretary, there are — and have been in government departments over the years — various patterns of behaviour. At one extreme there have been those secretaries who have sought to cling leech-like to the minister and to establish themselves as the only substantial source of advice, to be constantly at the minister's elbow and to discourage contact between the minister and other officers of the department. At the other extreme there have been those secretaries who have risked giving the minister the impression of deliberately keeping their distance, even perhaps talking down to him, and that they have their own distinct and unassailable power base. A bit like Sir Humphrey Appleby perhaps in *Yes Minister*. Most of us, though, probably came down somewhere in the middle.

The relationship between the minister, the secretary and the department is a three-way one — and in many cases as difficult as the classic eternal triangle. The initiative in handling it, in my view, should lie with the secretary. It is really up to the secretary to decide how he wants to present the department to the minister. I believed very firmly that, in most instances, I should encourage the minister to deal direct with senior officers on specific policy issues, especially those of particular complexity. If we had an expert on Japan, say, I thought it would be a waste of time for that officer to brief me and then for me to brief the minister. I thought the minister would be much better served by having direct contact with that officer and to be able to ask questions, to have a dialogue.

There were, of course, one or two angles to this. First, it was a deliberate act of delegation on my part intended to facilitate expeditious and effective handling of issues and to avoid bottlenecks. Second, it represented a deliberate expression of confidence on my part in the competence of individual officers, that I trusted them to have direct ministerial access, oral and written. I knew it would be on my head if any of them botched it. Although this did happen once or twice, it was a risk that, with most senior officers, I had little hesitation in taking. I also hoped that individual senior officers would respond positively to my demonstration of confidence in them.

Perhaps the best way of describing how I wanted the minister to see me in relation to the department — and I know this is a hackneyed analogy but I cannot think of a better one — was as the conductor of an orchestra playing *for his benefit*. I could not reasonably be expected to play every individual instrument with the skill of a professional player but I was responsible for the orchestra playing together and in tune.

But, if the minister's dealings were in many cases with senior officers, where did this leave me, as secretary? The answer, partly, lay in the arrangements I made within the department for making my own input to what was going on. I did this in various ways. To begin with I had regular morning meetings with a small group of senior officers. There the current and contentious issues were discussed. Then, time permitting, I discussed with individual senior officers by themselves, or accompanied by their own immediate offsiders, their major draft submissions to the minister. On major issues I would sign those submissions myself. I always saw drop copies of all ministerial submissions the day they were sent. If I thought it desirable I could always follow them up with the minister personally, either by seeing him or ringing him up, but it was rarely easy to make quick personal contact with most of the ministers I worked for. I return to this in a moment.

Then there was the daily intake of telegrams from overseas posts. The handling of telegrams has always been a major problem for any secretary. It certainly was for me. Every morning there was an enormous bundle of them, sometimes a foot or more high. I had a devoted assistant who used to come in very early and go through them all for me, picking out the ones she thought I should read, or at least be aware of. I felt I had to deal with the telegrams before the office opened properly at 8.30am. There was always the possibility of an early call about one of them from the minister or from the head of another department, say Prime Minister's or Defence, both of whom were early risers. And then, of course, there were the subsequent deliveries of cables during the day as well as the outward telegrams to be read, not all of them necessarily originating in Foreign Affairs.

There are two relevant points to be made. The first is that reading the telegrams was yet another and very important way of keeping up with events. The second is that the actual process of reading so much so quickly was a constant and severe physical strain. The reason Nick Parkinson had to retire as secretary was the damage being done to his eyes from having to undertake so much unavoidable reading, especially telegrams. In the end, he was told in mid-year that, if he kept that reading up, he would be too blind by Christmas to drive the car. Once he had left the job, his eye condition stabilised.

While I believed at the time that the arrangements I had made were the most effective I could devise to meet the minister's and the department's normal and regular working requirements, I have sometimes wondered since whether I should not have tried to be seen to be making more of a fuss of the ministers I worked for — to have been more conspicuously active in doing their bidding.

One practical problem, in regard to some ministers, was the difficulty of seeing them or securing an appointment, or even to talk on the telephone. In my day, especially when Parliament was sitting, ministers usually spent only three days of the week in Canberra. Often they found it impossible to spare time for appointments.

One quite common result was for me to spend a whole Monday or a Friday travelling interstate to see the minister on his home ground. If the minister was spending the week at home anyway, I had no problem, but I used to find it galling, when I knew the minister was coming to Canberra the following day or had flown home from Canberra on the afternoon of the previous day, to spend the whole day away from the office simply to have an hour or so, or even less, with him. And the expense to the taxpayer seemed unwarranted.

Relations with the minister could also be complicated by relations with the Prime Minister. Nick Parkinson told a meeting of the Australian Institute of International Affairs in Brisbane in 1992 how he was once rung by Prime Minister Fraser and asked a few questions, to which he gave the best answers he could. Shortly afterwards he was rung by an angry Mr Peacock asking him what he meant by going behind his back to the Prime Minister. I had similar problems on the home front.

One area of personal contact, both with the Prime Minister and the minister, was accompanying either or both on official trips overseas. In relation to prime ministerial visits, I often used to think of that wartime slogan: 'Is your journey really necessary?' There were times when I felt the departmental secretaries were there mainly for the sake of appearances and in case something happened that made us needed. On the other hand, the work of the prime ministerial Commonwealth Heads of Government Meetings, specially in the communiqué committee, was unremitting. All night sessions were common.

I have spoken of the secretary's role in relation to the Prime Minister and the minister. I now want to turn to Parliament. When Parliament was in session one of the daily tasks was to keep up to date for the minister the big file of draft answers to possible parliamentary questions (PPQs). The possible questions, and the proposed answers, had to be up-to-the-minute in content and over in Parliament House well ahead of Question Time to give the minister a chance to read them.

Often the answers amounted to brief and authoritative statements of Australian policy. It was here that I felt the secretary had an important role to play: to know what the minister had been told in previous PPQs and to be sure that the new formulations were accurate and succinct. Therefore, every day, or perhaps more accurately, every evening, I would go though the PPQs before they were sent across to Parliament House. I would, of course, be given the new ones, or the revisions, separately from the others already on file, but even so it was a time-consuming task. Often we had to make last-minute amendments because of some telegram that had just come in. There could be a real scramble under extreme pressure.

At times the secretary's role was to attend sessions of parliamentary committees and to answer questions. There were periods when ministers forbade their secretaries to attend those sessions, on the grounds that the secretaries could be seen as usurping ministers' roles in making and giving public expression to, matters of policy. At other times, the Opposition used the sessions to attack ministers through their private secretaries and other senior staff. That could be very uncomfortable. The discomfort was increased when the sessions were open to the press.

Another of the secretary's responsibilities, deriving mainly from the minister, was for relations with the Diplomatic Corps in Canberra. When a new head of mission arrived in Canberra, he or she presented credentials to the Governor-General at a formal ceremony at Yarralumla. There was provision in the order of proceedings for attendance by the minister. In practice, ministers very rarely went. That meant my getting dressed up in a morning suit and going to Yarralumla for an hour or two, often at the busiest time of day. Heads of Mission also expected the secretary to attend their national day receptions and to accept dinner and cocktail party invitations particularly when, as often occurred, ministers were unwilling or unable to accept invitations themselves.

I used to try to go to each diplomatic mission for dinner once a year. But that, coupled with the practice I had inherited of giving a formal farewell lunch in the department to every departing ambassador or high commissioner, plus the presentations, all took up scarce time. I did, though, have plenty of practice at making cheery little lunch and dinner party speeches for foreign diplomats. Those speeches would have been harder if I had not tried to establish good personal working relationships with the heads of mission themselves.

Our ministers have not been the first to shuffle off the corps. In 1900, Lord Salisbury delegated the work to a junior minister, telling Queen Victoria that 'many more ambassadorial afternoons would certainly shorten his life'. The same ministers, of course, often expect their representatives overseas to have instant high-level access to foreign governments. It is easy to forget the process is a two-way one.

I should like to turn now to the second half of the responsibilities I outlined at the beginning of this talk: the day-to-day management of the department as a large institution with a mobile and diverse membership. By and large, with the exception of the appointment of heads of mission overseas and the filling of very senior positions in Canberra, this did not involve most ministers.

Two headings come at once to mind: structure and staffing.

The structure of the department and of its overseas posts was the outcome of consultations with, and directives by, the Commonwealth Public Service Board. By this I mean the number of established positions and the salary scales applying to these positions, both at home and overseas. In addition the Board set allowance scales intended, theoretically, to cover the cost of living at overseas posts, such things as the education of children, the rental of living accommodation, excess medical expenses, etc. There was a system in force of regular Public Service Board (PSB) inspections of overseas posts as a preliminary to setting local allowances for each post. I use the word 'theoretically' advisedly. Things may be different and better now, but in my day the inequalities and vagaries of the allowance 'system' were notorious and most departmental officers had their favourite story about some PSB inspector who had little if any idea and did not seem to want to find out, what was involved in living and working in foreign countries. My favourite was the inspector who, after examining how we all lived and tried to make ends meet in Jakarta in 1956, stepped on the plane saying: 'I would never bring my wife to live here'.

If the Department believed an increase in staff was needed, whether for a section in Canberra or for an overseas post, it had first to convince the Board that a new position at a certain salary should be approved. Likewise, if allowances were thought to be inadequate anywhere in the world, the department had to take up the case with the Board. As you can imagine, these were laborious and time-consuming procedures.

The Board also had a key role to play in relation to departmental recruitment and departmental promotions. Again the actual procedures were laborious and time-consuming.

I mention all this about the Board simply to drive home the point that, when it came to managing the department and to establishing conditions of employment, the secretary was not the master of his own household. In later years, after I had left the public service and had in-depth contact with some major Australian companies, I used to reflect ruefully on the difference in circumstances between the limitations on me, as the head of a government department, and the freedom of action enjoyed by the chief executives of big commercial enterprises.

Against this background how did I deal with the personnel issues, with individual people and their conditions of employment? What were the major staffing and personnel issues facing me in 1979?

The biggest issue facing me, setting aside for the moment the conditions of service overseas, was how to begin bridging the gulf between the political staff of the department on one hand and the staff of the consular and administrative service on the other. The two career streams were quite separate and distinct, beginning with different recruitment procedures. The political staff were selected from university graduates on the basis of exhaustive selection procedures conducted in conjunction with the Public Service Board. The consular and administrative staff were clerical officers of the Commonwealth public service. The political staff could aspire to Second Division positions in the department in Canberra and to head of mission appointments overseas. There were no Second Division positions for the consular and administrative staff and none, as far as I knew, had ever been appointed a head of mission or a consul-general.

Some members of the political staff let their feelings of superiority show in a less than heart-warming way. Many of the consular and administrative staff exhibited varying degrees of resentment and ill-feeling. I strongly believed that this gulf should be bridged, that all members of the department had to feel they were members of the one team and that there should be no structural limitations on the advancement of competent people whichever section of the department they had begun their career in.

Now is not the place, nor is there time, to embark on a detailed account of steps taken by me in this area. Suffice it to say, though, that by the time I had left, some discernable progress had been made. Members of the consular and administrative service had reached the Second Division, had become Head of Mission and had become Consul General.

A related issue was the thorny question of lateral recruitment to the political side of the department. I did not like the idea of the department being a closed shop, or being criticised for it. I did not see why talented people who had not happened to be recruited at the usual age but who were keen to join and had something valuable to offer could not be brought in at middle or senior levels. This was particularly so when the person or people in question were already members of the Commonwealth public service.

The other side of the coin was that I felt it would be a good thing to promote the interchange of officers with some other government departments. It could broaden our outlook and theirs. I extended this also to having a limited exchange of staff with big Australian companies. I had valued my own six months secondment to (the Australian resources company) CRA, as it then was, and wanted to make it possible for others to have similar experience.

The prospect of even very limited lateral recruitment, which I believed I eventually achieved, aroused strong feelings amongst some of the political officers in the department who feared their career prospects were being threatened. Again, I cannot remember the details of how it went, but I do remember myself as acting secretary in 1977 when lateral recruitment was, I think, already an issue, microphone in hand, addressing a large lunchtime meeting outside the department. As I looked at the photograph in *The Canberra Times* next morning, I wondered if I had not crossed the borderline to becoming a politician.

Another group issue was the position of women in the department. Until the 1960s, Foreign Affairs, like all other departments, had been hamstrung by the *Public Service Act* requirement that female officers should resign on marriage. This meant that, by 1979, despite recruiting women graduates every year, the department was still suffering from the unsought loss of many members of a whole generation of female recruits — roughly from 1945–65. The reason why we had comparatively few senior female officers in 1979 was not prejudice against women, as the press and other critics tended to assert, but because so many good ones had, so to speak, 'gone missing'. With the passage of time and the continued recruitment of women graduates the gap has, I believe, now been filled. In 1979 it was a public issue which held no possibility of quick solution.

Before turning from groups to individuals I want to acknowledge the role played by a different but very important group of women, the secretarial staff of the Department. Both in Canberra and overseas much depended on their competence and good humour. Often they had to contend with very difficult places to live and work. Most did so uncomplainingly and made notable contributions to the department. As secretary I had regular contact with the head of that group.

I move now to individual staffing matters. I had to spend a considerable amount of time on making head of mission recommendations to the minister; on overseas posting decisions for other staff; on promotions and placements of all staff, specially at the more senior level; and on the recruitment of graduate staff. To do all this properly, I felt I should know personally as many as possible of those concerned.

The position was complicated by so many people serving overseas for so much of the time. So I instituted a system of having short personal interviews with all staff, both political and consular and administrative, from very senior down to about First Secretary or Class 8, either going to or coming back from a posting. I felt that, given the nature of the Foreign Service, individuals had a justifiable expectation of some personal exchange with the boss, even if it lasted no longer than 15 or 20 minutes and occurred only every three or four years. It also gave individuals an opportunity, if they wanted, to get matters of great personal importance to them off their chests to me, and it was invaluable background for me in the decisions I had to make about them.

There were also one or two people who have been mentioned by Sir Edward Woodward, the former Director-General of the Australian Security Intelligence Organisation (ASIO), in his recent autobiography, *One Brief Moment*.[7] Of Australian representatives abroad who were homosexual. Sir Edward wrote:

> I helped Peter with one difficult area of his responsibility ... On at least two occasions I interviewed the officers concerned and said that their security clearances were not at risk, provided they were open with us about their sexual preferences and they reported immediately any attempted blackmail. This was our concern, because a person who was in denial was very vulnerable. Peter made the final decision, but I was happy to back and reinforce his views in those cases where he judged the risk to be minimal.

The exercise of that responsibility, thankfully, did not come my way very often.

How many failures did I have in my attempts to get on terms with the staff of the department? I shall never know the answer to that question. There are two people, though, who come immediately to mind: the head of mission who brought a tape recorder with him to a private meeting between the two of us, saying he did not trust me to stick to what I told him; and the officer who refused to shake my hand when he came for a farewell call. Others, I know, have borne lasting resentment for my carrying out instructions from the minister affecting them and their careers. It was not simply, as I think they supposed, whether I believed, or did not believe, what they had told me, or whether I had failed to defend them effectively. I was not the one who had the last say.

One last area of responsibility I should like to mention briefly is relations with other departments and government bodies. As well as Foreign Affairs, there were two organisations responsible to our minister — the Australian Secret Intelligence Service (ASIS) and the Australian Development Assistance Bureau (ADAB). I found it important to have regular and effective contact with the heads of both. Then, in its own special category of proximity, there was the Public Service Board. There follow the major departments of state: Prime Minister and Cabinet, Defence, Trade, Treasury and Immigration. At the personal level, I believed I should try to get on well with my counterparts in those departments even when there were differences in view and outlook on matters under discussion.

The reasons for some problems with the Board have already been mentioned. Another factor in our relations with the Board and with other departments, was the widespread recollection of Alan Renouf's very public, but unsuccessful, attempts in the mid-seventies to have a separate foreign service act, like the *Trade Commissioners Act*, and broadly to allow Foreign Affairs to run itself. In many ways it was a logical and commendable objective but it was just not practical politics. But as a result of the attempt I was well aware that, in the eyes of many of my counterparts, Foreign Affairs could get above itself and needed sitting on.

Problems occurred with the Department of Trade from time to time, largely I think because of the differences between the Liberals and the Country Party within the Coalition when it was in power. I can remember only one major falling out with Jim Scully when he was secretary of Trade. I thought that Australian exporters would benefit from advice on local political factors within their target countries, especially in South East Asia, and that their executives would find it useful to call on heads of mission as well as trade representatives when they visited those countries and for heads of mission visiting Australia to call on them. Jim misconstrued this and thought that, in approaching individual companies, the department was trying to horn in on areas that belonged to Trade. The subsequent amalgamation between Foreign Affairs and Trade will have resolved that kind of difficulty, I hope.

In relation to Defence, there was a formal requirement for the secretary to represent the department at meetings of the Defence Committee. The Committee, which also included Treasury and Prime Minister and Cabinet, had very wide-ranging responsibilities to present policy options to ministers. Contrary to the impression of one or two ministers, the Committee's role was not to make policy, which would have been to usurp the role of ministers. I have been told that these ministerial views led later to the Committee being disbanded.

I have spoken of the role of the secretary in relation to the minister, Parliament, departmental staff and other departments. I have said nothing about the press. This has not been a deliberate omission but has come about because in my day, although I have had interviews with individual journalists from time to time, the regular contact with the press was undertaken first and foremost by ministers, who regarded it as their prerogative, and then on a lower level by the departmental Press Officer. Personally I never felt at ease with most members of the press. On one occasion, Michelle Grattan[8] rang me up at about 11 o'clock at night in Washington after I had had a very good and very liquid dinner with Nick Parkinson, then Australian ambassador there, to check some abstruse point on policy towards Cambodia. I still vividly remember agonising for the next few days over every Australian press summary from Canberra. Fortunately, I had got it right. But on that and many other occasions of press contact I never felt really comfortable.

So now, to conclude, I hope I have given you some idea of what I did and what I tried to do and some of the major difficulties I faced, in terms of running the department. It was a stimulating challenge that lasted five years most of which I enjoyed. I have always been glad I had the opportunity of taking it on.

I just wished at the time, though, that like Mrs Thatcher and Mrs Marcos at their much more elevated levels, I could get by on four hours sleep a night.

ENDNOTES

[1] *Independence and Alliance: Australia in World Affairs 1876-80*, P.J. Boyce and J.R. Angel eds, George Allen and Unwin, Sydney 1983.

[2] As Mr Henderson's was the first in the series of presentations, his address focuses more on the formal aspects of the role of departmental secretary, and somewhat less on the detailed policy issues with which he was involved.

[3] The appointment procedure prescribed under the *Public Service Act* 1976 means the Chair of the Public Service Board and two other heads of departments would be involved.

[4] Alan Renouf was secretary of the Department of Foreign Affairs from 1974-77. Sir Nicholas Parkinson was secretary of the Department from 1977-79.

[5] Minister for External Affairs, 1941-49.

[6] See Peter Edwards' *Arthur Tange: Last of the Mandarins*, Allen and Unwin, 2006.

[7] *One Brief Interval. A Memoir* by Sir Edward Woodward. Melbourne: Miegunyah Press, 2005.

[8] Veteran journalist in the Parliamentary Press Gallery and one-time editor of *The Canberra Times*.

Stuart Harris, AO

Secretary of the Department of Foreign Affairs, 1984–87, and Department of Foreign Affairs and Trade, 1987–88

Background

Stuart Harris was secretary through a time of considerable upheaval in the Australian Public Service: changes that also had a major direct impact on the Department of Foreign Affairs. From 1983, the Hawke Government instituted major reforms to the Canberra bureaucracy seeking to make it more performance oriented, better focused on client service and, generally, more efficient and effective. As secretary, Harris was determined to introduce these reforms into the department on the grounds that it could not remain aloof from such changes as it might have in the past.

The second upheaval resulted from the 1987 changes to the Administrative Arrangements that saw the Department of Trade broken up and all its external components brought into Foreign Affairs and renamed the Department of Foreign Affairs and Trade. As a former Deputy Secretary of the Department of Trade, Harris was well placed to oversee this transition, but the pressures that this generated cannot be underestimated. Eventually, this reform was regarded as a considerable managerial triumph and was emulated by some other foreign ministries. The reforms changed the culture of DFAT for at least the next two decades. Despite the 'pain' of absorbing budget cuts consistently over many years (often more than other departments in Canberra), the 1987 changes left the Department 'competitive' with its overseas counterparts.

Internationally, these were times of unusually rapid political, economic and technological change. Gorbachev's perestroika reforms in the Soviet Union, the growing success of China's 'open door' policies and transforming economic growth in the other 'newly industrialising countries' of East Asia, all had some impact on Australia. Managing Australia's alliance with the United States as the differences emerged between the relatively new progressive Labor Government in Canberra and a conservative administration in Washington, represented a particular challenge for the Department.

Australian diplomacy had to adjust to an increasingly globalised world, where issues were inter-related and where managing the implications of technological change confronted governments everywhere with difficult choices. While he was the first non-career diplomat to head Foreign Affairs in forty years,[1] as an economist, Harris was comfortable dealing with economic aspects of international relations that were increasingly impinging on traditional foreign policy concerns.

Stuart Harris was the author of the Review of Australia's Overseas Representation in 1985. Since his retirement as secretary, he returned to The Australian National University where he has written extensively about international affairs.

Harris Presentation 8 August 2006

On my first day at what was then the Department of Foreign Affairs, I naturally wondered, as one does, what aspect of Australia's role in changing the world, bringing about peace or at least stopping World War Three, I would be involved in as secretary of the Department.

Well, as it happened, on my first day I was involved in averting a potential *lock-out* by the union because of a dispute over asbestos found in some plumbing refurbishment in the basement of the Foreign Affairs building. My first instruction from the minister a day or two later was to stop the leaks of confidential cables to the press. My second ministerial instruction was to put an end to the queues outside the Sydney passport office that were featuring graphically in Sydney newspapers. I am pleased to say success was achieved in each case — but, although it had stood me in good stead, I did not expect what I thought of as my considerable experience in international negotiations — bilateral as well as multilateral — under J. G. Crawford and successive ministers including John McEwen and Doug Anthony, to be brought into play in this way.

The passport office exercise was an interesting one, in that Prime Minister Hawke subsequently brought in a consultant to improve governmental efficiency and his approach was, as is the approach of efficiency experts, to reverse whatever was in place. In this case, this meant undoing the changes we had made successfully to improve the operations of the Sydney office. We simply pretended to follow his instructions — and while I was not yet ready to lie for my country, I could at least lie for my new department.

Those experiences illustrate a point Peter Henderson made in his presentation — that being head of Foreign Affairs was substantially an administrative task and, particularly, one of managing the diplomatic network. I will refer to some of the administrative changes that I introduced as secretary — some of which have stayed, some not.

I was, of course, an outsider appointed to head the department, but I was given loyal support from most in the department and exceptional support from some, particularly Geoff Miller and Mike Costello and later David Sadleir.[2] I was appointed, partly, I imagine, because of the Government's interest in a greater economic focus; partly, again, because when I left the Trade Department, where I had been a deputy secretary, and went to The Australian National University,

I had been talking about the implications for Australia's governance of global changes that later came to be called globalisation. This seemed to me to have substantial implications for the way we operated in the world, not only in economic but also in political and security contexts.

In that context I had pointed to the logic of combining the trade and foreign affairs departments, provided internal policy debate remained strong. I was concerned, however, about the potential risk this created for suppressing internal debate within a combined department — as I still am.

Globalisation had, and still has, a great many consequences. Foreign relations were increasingly fragmented and diffused. The communication changes, for one, meant that the information process became much more open, with the media and elements of civil society (NGOs) often ahead of formal intra-government reporting. The 'bean-counters', in their unwisdom, saw the CNN factor implying a reduced role for the department — and therefore argued that we needed fewer resources. In practice, the department needed more resources to be able to analyse CNN-type reports — to confirm, to elaborate, to interpret and to respond — for the government. Growth in travel — by tourists, representatives of business and various non-governmental actors — also had an impact on Australia's foreign relations. This, together with the growing complexity of foreign relationships, put added demands not only on the head office in Canberra, but especially on its overseas representatives, who needed, particularly, to deepen their understanding of what was happening in their areas of responsibility. Environmental issues were becoming more salient (whales, Antarctica) as were human rights, and some bad phenomena were emerging, including diseases and crime, not all of which were as evident as they have since become, but were prevalent enough even then to need greater attention.

It was evident that, in managing international interdependence, policy-makers needed to operate in a wider variety of contexts, to link up more with other governmental and non-governmental actors and to respond to growing public interest in international issues. All of this was to have significant implications for foreign policy coherence. The reality was that a growing number of departments had international connections. Increasingly the gap between domestic and international policies was diminishing and would continue to do so. Many more departments had international units — desirably so — but this increased the importance of having a coherent international voice.

Part of the consequence of the increased competitive environment of globalisation was that Australia needed to speak with one voice — something it often did not do — and it was by no means just trade and foreign affairs that was involved. That was something that John Menadue, then head of Trade, and I sorted out quite amicably, as was to be the case later with Primary Industry with the help of the secretary there, Graeme Evans, and the minister, John Kerin. But, more generally, I resuscitated and renegotiated the Prime Minister's Directive to Australian Heads of Mission which affirmed the overriding responsibility of the Australian Ambassador as the senior governmental representative of Australia in any country.[3] That seemed to work well at the time and I assume that it is still in place.

I was asked by my minister, Bill Hayden, to undertake a review of the foreign service which the government had made a commitment to carry out. Although this would represent number ten, or so, of reviews of various aspects of the foreign service in recent years — usually designed to cut staff numbers — I took it seriously — as did the many departmental officers who helped me. The review tried to set out how, in the new international circumstances, foreign representation should operate efficiently and what that meant for overseas representation generally. Looking at it again recently, I was surprised at how well it stood up. It made a lot of recommendations based on the expectation — which I think has been borne out, and contrary to the superficial views of a lot of commentators — that globalisation would increase the demands on the external departments and not reduce them.[4]

The Minister for Finance at the last minute indicated to Hayden that he wanted the review to show where substantial cuts could be made. So that is what the review did, but it also showed what the consequences of any cuts would be. One of those has, in my view, become even more important — our increasing dependence on analyses and information provided from overseas by those whose interests often differ substantially from those of Australia.

I am second to none in my admiration for many aspects of the American system and society, but when the alliance is lauded for our access to US intelligence, one does wonder what this means when the intelligence was so wrong in guiding the decisions on the invasion of Iraq and subsequently.

We also assume, without critical thought, when we talk about sharing common values — and not just with the United States — that, when articulated, we attribute the same meanings for those values such as freedom and democracy. Yet such terms have gone beyond shared ideals to become ideological terms in the approach of political groups such as the neo-conservatives; they have been de-linked from reality, their meaning defined and simplified, imbued with absolute truth and pursued with passion.

My role in administering the department was a major one. Some changes that I thought important included more equity and transparency in promotions of personnel, re-establishing a critical policy planning process, increasing interaction with academics; introducing a policy roundtable mechanism for and by junior staff, and initiating a system whereby those in disagreement with a line being recommended to the minister by the Department could question it and, if necessary, have the alternative referred to the minister (it was never necessary to do so, but it helped to stop leaks) and supporting the independence of what is now AusAID and was then the Australian International Development Assistance Bureau (AIDAB). But administration was not my only function, so let me talk briefly about some of the substantive issues of the day.

In my time, the Prime Minister and (the Foreign Minister) Mr Hayden[5] had different interests and accepted that each would take the running in their own areas of interest in what was, nevertheless, and despite the recent history,[6] a professional and cooperative relationship. Thus the Prime Minister was particularly concerned, but not exclusively, with the United States, China, the Middle East, the Commonwealth and the South Pacific and also with international trade; Hayden was concerned with arms control, nuclear non-proliferation and disarmament, the United Nations and Southeast Asia, especially Indo-China. A particular role I had was to respond to the concerns of both in order to heighten Australia's economic priorities and to give overseas representation a more commercial focus.

Before joining the department I had been closely involved in the Asia-Pacific economic cooperation process with colleagues from the ANU, including Sir John Crawford and Dr Peter Drysdale in such developments as the Pacific Economic Cooperation Council (or PECC). Although the process had an ostensibly economic focus, it also had a large security overhang. In that context, Saburo Okita, the one-time Japanese foreign minister and I had discussed on several occasions the need for an official institutional process to follow up on the kinds of conclusions being reached in PECC. Discussions in Canberra took this further to become the embryo of the APEC proposal floated by Hawke in Korea shortly after I left the department.

My contact with Bob Hawke had begun when I was head of what is now the Australian Bureau of Agricultural and Resource Economics (or ABARE), then the Bureau of Agricultural Economics (or BAE). As head of the Australian Council of Trade Unions (ACTU), Hawke would ask for information to use in his annual basic wage cases. He was similarly concerned about Australia's slow reaction to global change. As head of the department, I would travel more with Hawke than with Hayden in order to maintain the communication link between the two when the Prime Minister was travelling. As part of the process of delegation of responsibility to Division Heads that I had introduced in the department, it was more appropriate that Mr Hayden, when travelling, should have with him the subject or area specialists, usually those responsible for the relevant geographic area.

I was involved therefore with the international aspects of the government's reform program, including moves to make Australia more market-oriented and the further development of relations with China, an interest of mine since my first official visit there in 1973. I was also concerned to raise the level of policy attention to Northeast Asia where I considered most of our future economic prospects — and our political interests — lay.

That I was more closely linked to the issues in which the Prime Minister involved himself was also partly a consequence of my previous background of international negotiations with multilateral institutions — such as the GATT, UNCTAD[7] and various other UN groups and in the regional cooperation processes; it was also because Mr. Hayden was a hands-on minister who was very involved and knowledgeable on the issues in which he was particularly interested and my direct and detailed involvement was less necessary.

The government at the time was multilaterally-oriented. This reflected the trend that, with globalisation, issues increasingly needed to be dealt with collectively in the international sphere — fewer and fewer issues could be dealt with by a country acting alone. Moreover, even where there was a choice, as with trade relations, economic analysis points to the greater protection for smaller countries in multilateral measures than in bilateral measures. The need for this is greater now than ever, which is why the current difficulties with the Doha Round are disturbing.

There was also an economic rationality bias among the ministers involved in international issues, not just the Trade and Foreign Ministers, but also including others such as the Treasurer, Finance Minister and the agriculture and resources ministers. The Prime Minister was particularly active in foreign policy, always wanting extensive briefing — which he read and remembered. He also held strong views that at times led to vigorous — indeed robust — argument in which you were expected to hold your own.

This was an interesting and important period of major change in Australia. The government's reform program was helped in practice by the support of the Opposition that made the reform program a largely bi-partisan one. In its first major step, the government freed up the exchange rate. More broadly, it moved away from what the journalist Paul Kelly referred to as 'the Australian Settlement': centralised wage setting, protection of industry, state paternalism and immigration.[8] The reforms opened up substantial opportunities generally and had significant international ramifications, most notably in the international trade context.

It was also a significant time internationally as, among other things, the Cold War moved to its close. Having closely followed developments in the Soviet Union for some time, I had given a conference paper talk in 1986, cleared with Hayden, saying Gorbachev should be taken seriously. This attracted strong criticism from the media and from some in Defence. It was a view, however, that Hawke took with him when we went to Moscow in 1987, despite criticism from the Opposition. We were eventually proved right.

Both the Prime Minister and the Foreign Minister were involved in different aspects of Australia's relationship with the United States. This was a time of suspicion and concern in Australia over the Reagan administration's attitude to nuclear war. The relationship became important for me in respect of the testing of MX missiles and especially in handling communications between the New Zealanders and Australia when New Zealand disengaged from the ANZUS treaty.[9] Despite some adverse implications for us, in practice our alliance value increased. But although the New Zealanders did not make it easy for us, it was important not to dump on the New Zealanders as there was no doubt a lot of public sympathy in Australia for the little guy, given the wide perception that the United States had over-reacted.

Other aspects of ANZUS were the regular meetings of defence and foreign ministers that, although symbolically important, were too formulaic to be very useful and would have gained from greater preparation and discussion rather than as the set pieces that usually eventuated. And yet, this was also a time when Australia had its own strong views on China and on the Asia-Pacific region. Perhaps surprisingly, the State Department in the Reagan Administration listened to and, indeed, sought, Australia's views on those issues. The State Department's Asian team under Secretary of State George Shultz and Gaston Sigur — and in the White House, among them Jim Kelly — was particularly strong.[10]

Even so, the US administration was singularly uninterested in our views on nuclear test bans. They were also unreceptive, moreover, when in the face of aggressive subsidised US competition consciously targeting Australia's agricultural markets in Asia and elsewhere, we put economic issues on the ANZUS agenda. These arguments were listened to politely but with absolutely no effect. Whatever our strategic importance, in compartmentalised US administrations, we were fair game for US economic interests — I do not think that has changed.

The 1980s was a difficult period for Australia's trade not only because the United States was targeting our agricultural export markets as, for a while, were the Europeans. The US-EU subsidy war forced world agricultural prices down generally. We also had problems in our resources trade with Japan. Japan was playing 'hard ball' on our coal and iron ore prices: the global economic downturn had led to an oversupplied market, to which Japan's own activities had contributed. Together with their unified negotiating tactics, this gave them a strong bargaining position.

At this time, we had frequent joint ministerial meetings with Japan and those meetings tended to revolve about resource trade issues. I had had a long experience in dealings — not always successful — with Japan, a country and people I like very much, and that experience was important in dealing with a situation where we had evidence that a major Japanese company had breached a firm Japanese prime ministerial commitment given to Australia. The choice was, as some suggested, confronting the Japanese authorities publicly with this information or taking an approach that saved the face of the responsible minister. After long discussion, under my urging and with Hayden's support, we took the latter course, resolving the issue but avoiding generating long-term resentment.

These ministerial meetings had been essentially economic in substance but, during this period, we started the first interchange with Japan on political issues, although these subsequently seemed to fall by the wayside until more recently. Not all ministers found the Japanese as easy to interact with as other countries in Northeast Asia, such as the South Koreans and the Chinese, and I often found it necessary to make the point that, difficult or not, Japan would long be the major market for our exports.

Commonwealth meetings at the time were mostly quite interesting since South Africa and apartheid was a central topic. Hawke was active in this environment, since his opposition to racism was deeply held. South Africa was also targeting Australia in trying to entice sports teams to visit South Africa to get around our sporting boycott policy. I felt we were losing the argument within Australia and first the minister and then I gave several public presentations that explained why that was a problem.

Robert Mugabe at this time was still running what was then a more or less showcase, tolerant country. One Commonwealth meeting, however, discussing a report on Africa, revealed differences between the British Foreign Secretary, Geoffrey Howe, and the Prime Minister, Margaret Thatcher, that, for more politically sensitive observers than I, were the kind of differences that ultimately led to her losing Britain's leadership. South Africa also brought Hawke and Indian Prime Minister Rajiv Gandhi close together and I will always remember Gandhi's extreme courtesy.

It was during the 1987 Commonwealth Heads of Government meeting in Vancouver that, after consultation with Jim Wolfensohn, then a New York banker, we fashioned an approach to financial sanctions on South Africa that, elaborated in detail by a Treasury officer, was subsequently judged influential in tightening substantially banking sanctions on South Africa's apartheid regime and contributed to its ultimate demise.

As I noted earlier, the Prime Minister's reform program included reduced tariff protection and this became an important part of the government's international agenda. The Uruguay Round was in its early stages and the promise by Hawke to lower tariffs and bind them was significant in restoring our substantially diminished credibility in the GATT negotiations. The full burden of the Uruguay Round came later after the two departments of Trade and Foreign Affairs were amalgamated.

This came in 1987 and, although I was consulted and agreed with the move, it was not my idea at this specific time. I could see its advantages, but I was worried about the costs and about how balanced the outcome would be. Some of the reasoning behind the change involved recollections of conflict, which although once undoubted, were largely a matter of past history, while other bureaucratic conflicts had emerged — such as those between the departments of Trade and Primary Industry. The perception of the Department of Trade having served as what was seen, not without justification, as a Country Party 'secretariat', remained in some ministers' minds and Trade had, as a consequence, been considerably reduced in size and had lost much of its effectiveness and clout.

We had very little time to prepare for the change, but I thought it important to make the change swiftly. By the formal date we had a new name on the building, new stationery and a new organisational structure in place. The specifics had been worked out cooperatively by working groups with equal representation of the two old departments — a very constructive bonding exercise.

Together with an outstanding group of senior colleagues — Philip Flood, Peter Field, Mike Costello and Mike Lightowler[11] — I was concerned that, although we acknowledged that two different departmental cultures existed, there was to be no 'we' and 'they' in the amalgamated department, the importance of which I had learned from the difficulties of the comparable Canadian amalgamation. I think we substantially achieved that and, to a large extent, this ceased to be a major issue.

There was a lot of stress, nevertheless. The Department of Finance had its own agenda of cuts of staff and functions that had been in their sights for a long time, such as the journalists of the Australian News and Information Bureau. We saved some of them — but far from all — and concerns about career futures became more widespread.

What the amalgamation did do was to enable us to perform much more effectively in the Uruguay Round with great economic benefit to Australia. It became possible to utilise the diplomatic network in particular — which responded positively. The great strength of the Trade Department was its culture of immensely thorough preparation for negotiations. It is almost certainly true that the Australian delegation was better prepared than any other delegation: it had detailed studies available to it from the BAE, which we fed into the negotiation process and were then taken up by the OECD; we chaired the new service sector negotiations; and Peter Field, the overall leader of the Australian delegation, was probably more knowledgeable and experienced on the issues than the leaders of other major delegations. With the backing that the Cairns Group and our ministers gave him, he became an important player in the negotiations. Unfortunately, Peter was taken seriously ill towards the end of the negotiations, in my view a consequence of the considerable stress associated with the negotiations, and could not complete them.

The Cairns Group itself was an important initiative from the Trade department. We were asked by the Minister for Trade, John Dawkins, to advise on its feasibility. I favoured it, but suggested that Hayden test it out on the ASEAN ministers that he would shortly be meeting — where the response was positive. As a coalition of the willing, it eventually proved especially effective as a 'third force' in the negotiations, despite problems with our Canadian colleagues that I had foreshadowed to Dawkins.

These are just some of the issues of the day that affected my role as secretary. Some of them, and others I have not dealt with, remain and many new issues have arisen. I think that the department is now potentially much better equipped through the amalgamation to deal with the range of current issues. I do wonder whether the less open atmosphere of the current public service enables that potential to be fully realised. And I do not see this 'less open atmosphere' as necessarily associated with an appropriate increase in ministerial control compared with earlier post-war decades. No-one would suggest that Hayden had anything but full control.

I certainly found a strong internal debate to be critical to getting things as right as one could. It was also what made the job so interesting. Without that interest, I suspect the really high level of intellectual capacity needed to advise ministers on how to pursue effectively Australia's national interest internationally will not stay in the department to rise to senior levels, but will be tempted to move out after a few years of developing contacts and gaining saleable experience.

Fortunately that was not a problem for me when secretary of the Department of Foreign Affairs and Trade.

ENDNOTES

[1] *Diplomacy in the Marketplace: Australia in World Affairs 1981-1990*, ed. By P.J. Boyce and J.R. Angel, Longman Cheshire, Melbourne, 1992.

[2] Miller, Costello and Sadleir served as deputy secretaries in the Department. At that time, there were three deputy secretary positions.

[3] This directive, signed by the Minister, was presented to each head of mission as they took up their assignment and was to be their mandate in their job. The directives were tailored to each country and each head of mission and, among other things, reaffirmed the head of mission's authority over officers from other departments who were stationed in the Australian mission.

[4] The *Review of Australia's Overseas Representation* was published by the Australian Government in 1985.

[5] Bill Hayden was Minister for Foreign Affairs from 1983-87, Minister for Foreign Affairs and Trade from 1987-88, and Governor-General from 1989-96.

[6] A reference to Hayden's removal as party leader by Hawke on the eve of the 1983 general election.

[7] GATT is the General Agreement on Tariffs and Trade, the predecessor of the World Trade Organisation. UNCTAD is the United Nations Conference on Trade and Development. Both organisations are based in Geneva.

[8] Paul Kelly, *The End of Certainty*, Allen and Unwin, 1992.

[9] New Zealand was suspended from ANZUS Treaty in 1985 after the New Zealand Labour Government under Prime Minister David Lange refused to permit visits by nuclear warships.

[10] Gaston Sigur and James Kelly were, successively, Assistant Secretary of State for East Asian and Pacific Affairs in the Reagan Administration. Kelly also worked on the National Security Staff of the Reagan White House.

[11] Deputy secretaries after the merger of Foreign Affairs and Trade, Lightowler and Field had come from the Department of Trade. For a period, DFAT also had an Associate Secretary, Geoff Miller, former Secretary of the Department of Primary Industry.

Richard Woolcott, AC

Secretary, Department of Foreign Affairs and Trade, 1988-92

Background

Richard Woolcott's tenure as secretary coincided with one of the most active periods of Australian foreign policy under Gareth Evans, who began what would become an eight-year term as Foreign Minister the day after Woolcott was appointed.

Several Australian policy initiatives were active simultaneously. They included Prime Minister Hawke's efforts to bring APEC into being, Evans's determination to contribute to the Cambodian peace process, the development of a security dialogue in the Asia Pacific region (which was to become the ASEAN Regional Forum), attempts to inject more substance into Australia's relations with Indonesia, and Trade Minister Michael Duffy's push to bring to a successful conclusion the Uruguay Round of Multilateral Trade Negotiations. Australia also pursued a more active role in the United Nations, the South Pacific and the Indian Ocean.

Clearly, the most significant external event during the period was the end of the Cold War. This required new policy approaches and enhanced cohesion between defence and security policies generally. For Australia, it meant paying attention to its alliance with the United States while enhancing self-reliance. The other major event was the first Gulf War in 1991 (involving the Australian Defence Force).

The department coped well with these demanding challenges during the period. It was also managing technological change in its overseas network, which underwent substantial upgrading during this period. Bedding down the amalgamated department's new organisation and culture continued to be a high priority. The absorption of the trade and information functions into the department came to be regarded as one of the main successes of the 1987 moves towards 'mega-departments'. In time, and after some questioning, it was judged a success by both major political parties and the National Party.

Woolcott's appointment as secretary came later in his career than may have been expected (he had declined to be considered for the position in 1973). He had already served in high profile Head of Mission positions, including a lengthy period as Australia's Ambassador to the United Nations in New York (1982–88), during which he represented Australia on the Security Council for two years.

So Woolcott was already comparatively well known in Australia, the United States and in the Asia Pacific region and was well placed to play a prominent role in the initiatives launched by Hawke and Evans. His relaxed style of leadership was suited to the demanding tasks facing the department and he was a popular secretary.

Richard Woolcott has published *The Hot Seat: Reflections on Diplomacy from Stalin's Death to the Bali Bombings* (Harper Collins 2003). He continues to be a regular commentator on foreign policy.

Woolcott Presentation: June 8, 2006

While there is a value in talking about the past for the sake of the historical record, I would have preferred to offer some views on present foreign policy issues, especially those which relate to some of the problems with which I am familiar such as relations with Indonesia, with the United States, Iraq and East Timor. But that is not the purpose of this presentation.

I was the 16th secretary, counting from when it was called the Department of External Affairs, which was established in 1901. I filled the office from 1988 until my retirement from the Australian Public Service in 1992. Unlike some of my predecessors, like Peter Henderson, and some of my successors, I was appointed after I had been serving in Indonesia, the Philippines and New York. Except for occasional visits I had been away from Canberra for these 13 years when I came back to take over the position of secretary. We used to have a saying in the public service, especially about promotions, that if you are out of sight, you are out of mind. I had expected to retire gracefully after my posting in New York and was surprised when I was telephoned by the then Foreign Minister, Bill Hayden, and asked to come back.

How did I obtain the job? I really do not know. Looking around I see friends and colleagues who might well have been secretary of the department, in addition to the two who were. Good fortune, or simply being in a particular place at a particular time, together with the interaction of personal situations often entirely outside one's control and, indeed, the chemistry between senior personalities involved in the decision-making process, can all play a major role in such appointments.

I was fortunate to return to Canberra at a particularly active and challenging time. Usually there is a broad continuity in the way that Australian foreign policy is set, but 1988–89 was one of those defining periods; a watershed in world events that caught many ministers and officials by surprise. At the outset of my time the two great challenges of the previous four decades — that of communism and Soviet imperialism — were being simultaneously overcome. At the end of the Cold War there was a major shift in emphasis from global political and strategic issues to economic considerations.

Richard Woolcott, AC

In our own region, 1989 was the year that the Asia Pacific Economic Cooperation forum (APEC), a major Australian initiative, was established. It was also the year in which the Cambodian peace process and the regional security dialogue, which lead to the ASEAN Regional Forum (ARF), in both of which Australia played a leading role, were launched. So I found myself returning at an extremely interesting but also very active and demanding time.

Shortly after my return to Canberra in August 1988, I had a long private meeting with Prime Minister Bob Hawke. I am not sure that other prime ministers took the same interest as Mr Hawke did in the management of departments, but I was to assume duty on 1 September 1998, which was the day before Gareth Evans became Foreign Minister. So, unlike my predecessor Peter Henderson, I had one Foreign Minister right through my period and I am sure that is a much easier situation to deal with than having a number.

Bob Hawke told me that my first priority would be to see that the amalgamation of the two departments — Foreign Affairs and Trade — was made to work effectively. He used the interesting phrase that it had been a 'shotgun wedding', which would never have taken place if a bureaucratic committee had been established to deal with the pros and cons of such a merger. But he argued that it was logical and common sense for the foreign and trade policies of an essentially trading nation situated in East Asia to be closely coordinated.

Secondly, he said that Australia had performed well on the United Nations Security Council in 1985–86. We were now a middle-sized power that had a good measure of international respect and we should be playing a more positive role in regional diplomacy, once the administrative amalgamation was bedded down.

Finally, I was somewhat taken aback when he said that my new Foreign Minister, Gareth Evans, who would be starting the next day, would be on a sharp learning curve and that I would need to 'keep an eye on him', an unusual role for the secretary. He said that Gareth was a man of enormous drive and powerful intellect, which I was to discover was absolutely right. But he also thought that he was somewhat driven and there might be times when he would need steady advice. That is really the role of any secretary. Even so, I thought this was a rather interesting introduction to the job.

My first objective as secretary, apart from what Bob Hawke had spelt out, was to bring together the cultures of the formerly quite distinct departments, which had only recently been amalgamated. The Trade people felt they would be swamped in the larger Foreign Affairs Department. The Foreign Affairs people suspected that the Trade tail might wag the dog. My initial objective was to try and bring those distinct cultures together. I was probably at an advantage having been overseas for so many years, because I had not been part of the Canberra bureaucratic infighting which may have preceded my appointment.

My next task was to try to re-define the department's priorities in pursuit of Australia's national interests in the rapidly changing world of the final decade of the 20th century, particularly with a new Foreign Minister taking up duty at this time. Thirdly, I wanted to develop a stronger sense of teamwork and esprit de corps in the amalgamated department and, also, I particularly wanted to improve communication within what was now a larger organisation than it had been.

Then, of course, there was the issue to which Peter Henderson devoted quite a bit of his lecture and that is the need to ensure effective management of a large department in times of increasing financial stringency and accountability.

Also, I was not going to flinch from giving the two relevant ministers the best professional advice available. All ministers say they want frank and fearless advice, but my experience is that in reality few do, particularly if that advice runs counter to what they themselves might want to do, or what they think might be unpopular in a domestic political context.

As if those internal tasks were not enough, my period as secretary encompassed a number of remarkable events which created great volatility in the international situation — the Berlin Wall was demolished and Germany was reunited, symbolising the end of the Cold War. Gorbachev had introduced perestroika and glasnost, marking the retreat from Marxism and Leninism and inadvertently precipitating the disintegration of the Soviet Union, thus playing a major part in bringing the Cold War to an end. Then, of course, we had the first Gulf War in 1991, which followed Saddam Hussein's invasion of Kuwait.

I found the secretaryship at this time hugely demanding, being responsible for foreign policy advice not only to Gareth Evans, but also to the Minister for Trade, Michael Duffy. On top of that, Bob Hawke as Prime Minister had a close interest in foreign affairs and occasionally wanted direct advice.

In 1988–89 the Department had a budget of $1,304 million — a substantial budget — and a total staff in 1988 of some 5,000, including locally engaged staff overseas, as well as 90 overseas posts. There were times when I wondered whether I, or for that matter anyone else, could handle the job effectively. I was 61 years old when I took up the post and I asked myself whether I had the physical stamina and the intellectual energy for the work required, especially with such an active Foreign Minister. I even wondered, privately, whether I would fail the task and become an example of the 'Peter Principle' — someone promoted to a level above his or her competence.

In 1989 the department faced what I considered to be an unusually demanding situation, because in addition to the issues I have already mentioned, Gareth Evans, whom I believe history will judge to be our most active Foreign Minister, had launched four new initiatives. In addition, the Prime Minister had launched a major initiative — all of which proved to be very time consuming and a real problem for the department in trying the handle them simultaneously.

The Prime Minister had launched the initiative to bring APEC into being. Gareth Evans was determined to make a major contribution, both to the Cambodian peace process and the development of a regional security dialogue. He also wanted to put a lot of effort into what he called getting more 'ballast' or substance into our very important relationship with Indonesia. Moreover, Michael Duffy, the Minister for Trade, was determined to bring the Uruguay Round of multilateral trade negotiations to a successful conclusion, which would include new benefits for Australian agriculture.

How were we to deal with such an extensive agenda? I decided the only way to handle it properly was to delegate as much as possible. I remember I once went into the office of one of my predecessors, Keith Waller[1], and noticed his desk had no paper on it. I made the throwaway comment saying that I was surprised to see his empty desk. His reply was: 'My boy, I always regard an officer's intelligence as inversely proportional to the amount of paper on his desk. The secret of this job is delegation.' It is something which has stuck in my mind.

What we decided to do was to give the deputy secretaries specific tasks. Besides the amalgamation process, I focused on Mr Hawke's request to bring APEC into existence. Michael Costello, then a deputy secretary and later to be secretary, worked tirelessly on Cambodia.[2] The late Peter Field devoted himself almost full time to trade facilitation and liberalisation through the Uruguay Round. And Costello and I gave special attention to paving the way for a regional security dialogue. The other deputy secretaries, Michael Lightowler, Dick Smith[3] and Paul Barrett, who later became secretary for Defence, dealt with the other general duties.

I now want to touch on an issue that was raised in Peter Henderson's contribution, as an example of what can be the political aspects of the job. I was concerned to hear rumours that the Opposition was sceptical about the amalgamation of Foreign Affairs and Trade and was considering reverting to two separate departments should it regain power at the 1990 election. So, with the amalgamation under potential political threat, I decided it would be useful to talk to the Leader of the Opposition, Andrew Peacock, and the then leader of the National Party, Charles Blunt.[4] It is not appropriate for a secretary to undertake such activities with an opposition party without clearing it with his minister and I did that.

It turned out to be very productive in that Peacock was persuaded that it would be foolish to try to 'de-amalgamate' the departments. Blunt's view was different — he wanted to keep an open mind on it depending what portfolios his party might get if the Coalition won the election. Anyway it was all, in a sense, water under the bridge, because the Government was returned and the situation of confronting this question did not arise. I do feel, however, that had the government changed, the department would have remained amalgamated and I had taken the right course in dealing with this delicate political consultation.

As secretary, I decided to pay considerable attention to the appointment of Australia's representatives overseas — ambassadors, high commissioners and consuls general. From the sidelines I had witnessed a number of poor appointments which had contributed little to Australia's international standing and some which had even damaged our international reputation. Such appointments were usually politically motivated, but some career officer appointments were not as effective as they should have been.

It is quite clear that it is prerogative of the Minister for Foreign Affairs to make such appointments and no secretary would question that. Gareth Evans normally requested two or three names to be put forward by the secretary for each post, even if he had a person in mind for it. It was then left for the minister to consult the Prime Minister on the appointments to some of the major posts, usually Washington, Tokyo, Beijing, Jakarta, the United Nations and — for reasons mainly related to prestige and to our history — London.

I understand that this situation has since changed. My understanding is that the Prime Minister now [John Howard, at the time of Woolcott's lecture] wants to approve all appointments, even those to our smallest posts. This seems to me to be a means of complicating the appointment process and reducing the authority of the Foreign Minister.

I approached the issue of appointments with three main aims: Firstly, I wanted to resist political appointments, many of which did not serve Australia's diplomatic interests and could undermine morale in the career service if there were too many. There were six non-career heads of missions when I became secretary, including those in London, The Hague, Dublin, Wellington and New York. I derived some satisfaction from the fact that all of these had been replaced by career officers when I retired and there was only one non-career appointment overseas by March 1992. One of the reasons for this change was that Gareth Evans took quite a strong stand against political appointees who he did not feel would do the job effectively.

Some political appointments were successful and served Australia very well, like Sir Robert Cotton[5], who was both an excellent Consul-General in New York and an effective and popular Ambassador in Washington. On the other hand, Senator Vincent Gair — the former Leader of the Democratic Labor Party — was not a success.[6] Gough Whitlam imagined that, by moving him out of the Senate in 1974, he would get control of that chamber. I have to say I was really surprised when visiting Dublin in 1974 to hear some of the tales that were widely circulating in the city at that time about Mr Gair.

My second aim was to ensure that recommendations for appointments, which I put to the minister, were the best qualified and most suitable officers available for the particular posts. My third intention was to recommend more female officers on the basis of merit for Head of Mission appointments in what for years had tended to be a male-dominated area. That is not necessarily the fault of my predecessors or previous ministers, because for a long period of time a career female diplomatic officer was obliged — quite wrongly in my view — to resign if she got married. I was disappointed that, when I retired, we had only two female Heads of Mission, but it would not be long before that number could be substantially increased.

An initiative adopted during my period as secretary was to have a ministerial directive prepared for each newly-appointed Head of Mission. These were prepared at a senior level, vetted by me and signed by the minister. Their purpose was to set out for the Heads of Mission at the beginning of their assignments, the objectives to which they would be expected to work during their appointment and the major issues with which they would be expected to deal. There were, of course, unpredictable issues, but it was the extension of a process aimed at ensuring our Heads of Mission overseas were properly informed about policy thinking in Canberra and better equipped to make an input into the policy formulation process. This went back to 1971 when the then secretary of the Department, Keith Waller, and deputy secretary, Mick Shann, established the Policy Research Branch, which I returned from Ghana to head at that time.[7]

We also introduced the Department's first Corporate Plan to cover the period 1990 to 1993, which was launched jointly by Gareth Evans and Neal Blewett, who was then the Minister for Trade Negotiations. It smacks a little of managerialism, but it was a useful tool. It set out three-year programs for bilateral relationships and trade relations and, while I was initially a little sceptical about its value, it did turn out to be quite useful.

I was, as I have noted, secretary during the first Gulf War. It is instructive to compare our involvement then with our participation in the American-led invasion of Iraq in 2003. Of course, the war added significantly to the pressures on the department. How does one handle this sort of situation? I established a departmental task force in a special operations room that was open round the clock and led by Ric Smith, a calm and able officer who later became secretary of the Department of Defence.

I think Mr Hawke's handling of the Iraq situation was considered and constructive. He invited me as secretary to attend some of the meetings he had with the cabinet sub-committee he had established to deal with the war. This committee included Paul Keating, Gareth Evans, Senator Robert Ray and Senator

John Button.[8] With the decision to make a contribution to Operation Desert Storm virtually made, I saw my role as one of bringing possible foreign policy ramifications to the notice of Senator Evans and the Prime Minister. I said that we had a clear case of aggression by one member of the United Nations against another and it would be useful nevertheless — because the situation involved the Middle East — to explain our policy, preferably in advance, to those countries in South East Asia which had Islamic majorities including Indonesia, Brunei and Malaysia, as well as those with important minorities — the Philippines, Singapore and Thailand — and suggested to Bob Hawke that he stress the Australian Government had no hostility towards Islam; that the military campaign was purely an exercise to repel aggression.

In retrospect, I believe Bob Hawke's and Gareth Evans's approach was eminently sound, especially as it was the first time that Australian forces would be committed overseas since Vietnam. The Prime Minister himself briefed all the Middle Eastern Ambassadors and the announcement was delayed for about 12 hours while our Heads of Mission in South East Asia informed the foreign ministers of those countries. I believe this was a sound approach. It was an approach which, unfortunately, was not followed, as far as I know, when Australian forces were committed to the invasion of Iraq in 2003.

I think in fairness to officials who were involved during this period, there was a substantial difference between the situations of 1991 and 2002–03. Senior officials and the heads of intelligence organisations were dealing with a decision already taken at the highest level between the Prime Minister and the President of the United States in 2003. The role of the bureaucracy and the intelligence organisations was therefore reduced to one of implementation.

I am going to say something about the European Bank of Reconstruction and Development, really as an example of how the secretary needs to be a 'jack of all trades'. The secretary of the Department of Foreign Affairs and Trade was the alternate Governor to the Treasurer on the Bank's board.

The Treasurer, then Paul Keating, telephoned me and said he was going to go to the inaugural meeting of the European Bank of Reconstruction and Development, but he could now not attend. As I was the Deputy Governor I would need to go in his place. So I got on a plane, flew to London, made a speech and flew back. I worked out when I got back to Canberra that I had been in the air for much longer than I had been at the conference. So even with the advantages of modern air travel, situations are not always as attractive as they might seem to be.

I decided shortly after I became secretary that we should have a Management Information Report (MIR). We already had a highly classified Policy Information Report (PIR), which I had launched in 1971 in order to keep Heads of Missions in the field involved in the policy process in Canberra. So the Management

Information Report (MIR) was introduced. Senator Hill was participating in a Senate Estimates Committee hearing and he asked me what the MIR was about. I said that I had always believed — and my predecessors and successors would probably accept this — that an effective Department, or for that matter an effective Australian Mission abroad, must rest on a sound and competent administrative footing. I believed that good management is critical to the effectiveness of the department. That was the theme we used in the Management Information Report to keep our people updated on managerial changes and issues.

The conduct of Australian foreign policy is a continuing process and the secretary, together with his senior support staff, has a major role in advising ministers on a wide range of political and administrative issues. Officials do not make policy, although the myth is sometimes perpetrated in the media that they do. Ministers are responsible for policy decisions.

I found that one of the satisfactions during my time was observing younger officers grow into the task of understanding our external interests and our role in the wider world. I was enormously impressed by the qualifications, intelligence and dedication on the part of many of the younger officers and I could not escape the feeling that they were probably better qualified than my generation for the jobs they were going to do.

It is really for others, not for me, to judge how the department worked during my period in charge. People tend to gloss over the shortcomings and accentuate the merits of the about-to-retire and the newly dead. When you embark on a job like the secretaryship, you start off wanting to build some sort of highway to the future, but I am afraid that we all end up mending a few potholes and hoping that one day successors, other officers, will complete the highway.

In conclusion, all I can say is that it was an exacting, demanding and extraordinarily interesting position and, despite the strains, the long hours and the pressures it imposes on families, I felt honoured to have been given the opportunity to do something for this country and its people. I did my best to achieve the tasks the Government had set for the department, together with those I had set for myself. I do not think one can do more than that.

One final point I want to make in closing is that the officers of the department, despite the enormously increased pressures on them, responded very creditably to those pressures at all levels during my period in charge between 1988 and 1992.

Question: Were cables sent back by Missions overseas given sufficient weight?

This is always an issue. In any particular post you have a better grip on what is happening in that country. In Canberra, the minister, his officers and the department are looking at the whole picture, not just one aspect of it. So I think it is an important part of the Head of Mission's role to keep pushing the issues of concern to his own area particularly when they are going to impinge on Australian foreign policy.

I am not in a position to comment on the 'culture of compliance', which many say has grown up in the public service. It certainly was not the case during the period I am talking about. The best thing people in the field can do is to continue to put their cases. I do not know whether that is done so much now because of modern technology. E-mails have tended to replace cables; the telephone can be used if you want to say something you may not want recorded.

I have done that myself. I remember that in Indonesia when Malcolm Fraser became the caretaker Prime Minister after Gough Whitlam's dismissal, he sent a message to President Suharto which he wanted me to give to him without any publicity. I arranged to do this at his house, but there was a phrase in the message that I had doubts about. This was to tell the president that Fraser wanted to have the same sort of close relationship that Gough Whitlam had developed and Australia would like to see a solution to the East Timor problem in terms of Indonesia's interests.

I sent a telegram back saying that President Suharto would probably ask what this meant. I said the Government's policy had always been that the use of force could not be condoned and I presumed that in a caretaker situation that would remain, but it was not in the message. There was silence from Canberra, so I telephoned John Menadue, who was the secretary of the Department of the Prime Minister and Cabinet. After 24 hours he rang back and said the Prime Minister had said the words stand on their own merit and they were not to be interpreted by the Ambassador.

I saw Suharto and he asked what the phrase meant. I said, under our constitution, existing policy is not changed by a caretaker government and our policy is that the use of force cannot be condoned. I realised that I had exceeded my instructions and I did not have the guts to put it in a cable. E-mails did not exist then, so I telephoned the late Graham Feakes, who was then Head of the South East Asian Division, and told him what I had said and suggested he might endorse the file to this effect for the record.

Question: Do you consider that three years is an optimum period to be secretary? It would be considered an incredibly short period for the chief executive of a large bank.

The period depends on the individual. Health and age can be factors. You have someone like Sir Arthur Tange, who was secretary first of External Affairs and then of Defence for a total of about 21 years, with an interval of five years as High Commissioner in New Delhi.[9] On the one hand, you have the value of accumulated experience but, on the other, depending on the pressures, a danger of burnout. When Sir Keith Waller retired, I asked why he was going and he said, 'If I stay in this job another year it will kill me.' When I was secretary I became more aware of what he had meant.

Three years is too short. Perhaps four is right, although I would suggest not more than five. Things were different in the past. Senior public servants had somewhat more influence, the pace was slower and the problems less complex. You also need to think of opportunities for the younger up-and-coming officers.

Question: There is a general impression that in the last 10 years the Australian Public Service has become not a service of the public, but a ministerial service. Do you think there has been this change in Foreign Affairs?

The people here today who are in Foreign Affairs are probably able to give you a better answer. What happens, when a Government has been in office for a long time and with senior officers now on contract, is that there is a general reluctance to be the harbinger of bad news.

You have seen that in the 'Children Overboard affair'. You have seen it more recently with the Australian Wheat Board. In the case of the Wheat Board there are only two possible explanations for what happened. The idea of amalgamating Foreign Affairs and Trade was that the differences between trade policy and foreign policy would be solved under the one roof. Yet here you have a situation where the interests of a former government agency, recently privatised, is to protect the wheat market in Iraq. At the same time the Prime Minister and the Foreign Minister were preparing to invade Iraq.

It seems extraordinary that the Prime Minister, the Minister for Trade and the Foreign Minister never saw any of the warning messages. One explanation is that they may not be telling the whole truth; the other is that there has been a measure of reluctance to ensure ministers saw the messages they should have seen. I would have thought the ministers' staffs would have taken the cables and said, 'you need to look at this'. When ministers say they get thousands of cables a day and they can't look at them all, that is true, but the role of ministerial staff is to make sure they see those they need to see.

You hear about the culture of compliance, that staff do not want to pass on bad news. It also enables plausible deniability by ministers. I do not know if this is true but, if it is true, it is unhealthy.

Steady Hands Needed

Question: There has always been tension between the departments because of the different focus and interests. Could you tell us what was the issue that caused you most trouble in that regard and did you think the inter-ministerial mechanisms that were in place in your day were sufficient to cope with this.

This sparks a thought on which I should have focused. During my period there really were no great tensions. We had a mechanism — I do not know whether it still exists — that we called the policy coordination meeting. That consisted of the secretary and the deputy secretaries meeting with the Minister for Foreign Affairs and the Minister for Trade and their respective chiefs of staff. We would go through current issues. Normally someone from the Prime Minister's Office would sit in on that too. The whole purpose of it was to see that responses to issues were coordinated. Whilst there were some fairly robust arguments from time to time, it seemed to be a very effective mechanism in preventing the problems you are talking about.

Question: What were the highlights of your career, both as secretary and before you were secretary?

There are always highs and lows in any job. I suppose the highlights were the successful establishment of APEC in 1989 and, before that, representing Australia on the UN Security Council in 1985–86. On APEC, I was in Canberra at the time. I tended to accompany the Prime Minister on overseas visits, but when Mr Hawke went to Korea, I did not accompany him because Gareth Evans was away in Washington. That was when Mr Hawke launched the idea of an Asia Pacific Economic Consultative forum on the good grounds that the world was in danger of breaking up into three financial blocs — the Deutschmark bloc, a Dollar bloc and a Yen bloc — and Australia would be marginalised.

Canberra diplomatic missions were ringing me up and all the journalists were ringing me up and asking what this was all about: a huge new initiative out of the blue over lunch in Korea. Gareth Evans was also quite angry because he was in Washington and, because of the time difference, Jim Baker[10] who was the US Secretary of State, knew about it while Evans did not.

Baker was angry, asking how could Australia take this major initiative without even consulting America, even excluding the United States from the list of participants? So I prepared a note, outlining what needed to be done to convince the ASEAN countries they were not going to be marginalised. We needed to consider the status of America, also that of China, Taiwan and Hong Kong. There were a number of difficult issues to be resolved.

Mr Hawke made the announcement in January 1989 and the first APEC Ministerial meeting took place in Canberra in November of that year, so we took only 11 months to get a really major and, initially, somewhat criticised, initiative up and running, which I think has been very valuable to Australia. Every so often people say that it is moribund, but it is not. APEC has achieved much and it is still doing a lot of practical, useful things for the business community, such as harmonising customs regulations. So I suppose, if I were to identify a high point, it would APEC.

Another highlight of my career was helping to secure Australia's election in 1984 to the UN Security Council with a then record majority. I then had the honour to represent Australia on the Council for two very active and stimulating years. That was a demanding but essentially successful exercise. I feel we advanced Australia's standing at the United Nations.

It is strange but I feel I am becoming like a British colonial governor — an extinct species — because I was our last representative on the Security Council. We have not been on it since 1986 and it does not seem we can get elected in a secret ballot at present, unless we can secure an uncontested spot. This is not good for our standing in the United Nations and I hope this situation will change in the future.

ENDNOTES

[1] Sir Keith Waller was secretary of the Department of External Affairs from 1970-73.

[2] An authoritative account of the negotiations with Cambodia, including Michael Costello's role, is contained in Ken Berry's 'Cambodia - from red to blue: Australia's initiative for peace', *Studies in World Affairs*, Australian National University, Department of International Relations, 1997.

[3] Richard J. (Dick) Smith was Deputy Secretary of DFAT from 1988-1991and, later, Australian High Commissioner to the UK 1991-94.

[4] Charles Blunt, Member for Richmond (1984–90), was Leader of the National Party from 1989–90. He lost his seat in the 1990 election.

[5] Sir Robert Cotton was a former Liberal Party Minister for Industry and Commerce (1976–78) who served as Australian Ambassador to the United States from 1982-85.

[6] Vincent Gair, Senator from Queensland, served as Ambassador to Ireland from 1972–74, after leading the Democratic Labor Party from 1964-73.

[7] Sir Keith Shann became Ambassador to Tokyo (1974–77) before serving as Chairman of the then Public Service Board (1977–78).

[8] Robert Ray was Defence Minister at the time and John Button was Leader of the Government in the Senate.

[9] Sir Arthur Tange served as Secretary of the Department of External Affairs from January 1954 to April 1965 (11 years and two months) and as Secretary of the Department of Defence from March 1970 to August 1979 (nine years and seven months).

[10] James Baker was Secretary of State in the George H. Bush Administration from 1989–92.

Michael Costello, AO

Secretary, Foreign Affairs and Trade, 1993–96

Background

Michael Costello was secretary in the last years of the Keating Labor Government, years characterised, above all, by an intensification of Australia's engagement with Asia. This ambition for more comprehensive relationships with Asia was occasioned partly by the end of the Cold War but was also generated by the need felt by Australia — along with most other countries — to define its role in the new global order. The debate about civilisation and values sparked by Samuel Huntington's 1993 'Clash of Civilizations' article was a foretaste of the challenges of terrorism and the 'rise' of Islam.[1]

Internationally, this period marked some high points and low points for multilateralism. It not only featured the completion of the Uruguay Round of Multilateral Trade Negotiations, but also the emergence of unprecedented regionalism around the world: in Europe (the 1992 Maastricht Treaty); in North America (the 1993 NAFTA Agreement); and in the Asia Pacific (APEC's first summit was in 1993). Tragically, it was also the time of the break-up of Yugoslavia and the aftermath, including the United Nations mixed record in humanitarian intervention and nation-building.

Costello was secretary of the Department of Industrial Relations at the time of his appointment to head DFAT. He had previously been, for several years, deputy secretary of the department and had also served as Australian Ambassador to the United Nations in New York. He had played a prominent role in negotiating the Cambodia Peace Agreement on behalf of Foreign Minister, Gareth Evans, personally undertaking what was perhaps Australia's first example of 'shuttle diplomacy'.

During this period, the Department of Foreign Affairs and Trade and Costello himself, were directly involved in Australia's pro-active approach to Asia. Yet departmental management continued to be strained by expectations that 'DFAT would do more with less'.[2] Costello was comfortable with both his policy and managerial responsibilities. The Howard Government's summary dismissal of Costello, along with five other departmental secretaries, when it took office in March 1996 was much later described by journalist Paul Kelly as 'the greatest blood-letting upon any change of government since Federation'.[3]

Since leaving DFAT, Michael Costello has, amongst other things, been active as a commentator on national and international affairs for *The Australian* newspaper, while also working as CEO of ACTEW, the Australian Capital Territory's electricity and water authority.

Costello Presentation: 8 November 2006

I last spoke to the Institute of International Affairs on the 23 February 1995. I have nothing but fond memories of this Institute. Even so, I was reluctant to speak here today. First of all, I am quite concerned about these occasions. The trouble with former heads of this and bosses of that is we feel deep down that we were giants in our time and everything has 'gone to the dogs' since we left. We tell old 'war stories' and we regale ourselves about how the young chaps of the day cannot measure up and, of course, none of that is true. So I hope I avoid that in this presentation.

Another reason, which is a very practical one, is that I did not leave the department in the familiar way of most secretaries. That is, I did not retire with accolades all round. Along with five of my secretary colleagues at the time, I was sacked in 1996 by the incoming Government.

Fortunately, I did not have an individual contract, so that I could leave in some sort of order. Some of my colleagues were told on Thursday evening or Friday morning that their time was up and they had to hand in their car keys and leave by lunchtime. It was one of the truly ugly occasions of my working life. This did not happen to me only because I had not signed an individual contract. I had stayed with the more traditional way of doing things. This is a long lead-up to what is basically an excuse. I have a full-time job. After I left DFAT, I went to work as deputy managing director of the Australian Stock Exchange until 1999 when I joined Kim Beazley (then Leader of the Opposition) as his chief of staff.

After the election of 2001, I was — in those beautiful words — 'between engagements', 'resting' for about 18 months. Then I became managing director of ACTEW Corporation. Most of you will be familiar with seeing my ugly face on television at various times asking you to use less water. That has been a surprisingly stimulating and interesting job and certainly a full-time one when I add it to my other directorships and writing a weekly column for *The Australian*.

Again, this is a long way of saying that I have not had time to write a carefully worded speech, the kind of excellent and thoughtful review of my time as secretary that you have heard from Peter Henderson and Dick Woolcott, and I have not had the time to access the records. So today I am doing this from notes. I cannot claim to be like Sir Arthur Tange, who used to speak from four dot points and produce perfectly parsed sentences. And certainly not as well as Gareth Evans who could deliver not just perfect sentences off the cuff, but perfect paragraphs. But I will do my best.

Michael Costello, AO

I will talk about a few of the big Departmental issues from my time as secretary — issues, which I feel are still important and major today — to see where they have gone. I will also touch on a few of the big policy issues which were around at that time and reflect on where they stand today: to see what is different and to see if there are any general conclusions to be drawn.

What are the Departmental issues? Dick Woolcott was the secretary who had to implement the integration of the Departments of Foreign Affairs and Trade. He took that very hot potato and lobbed it in my direction, along with Michael Lightowler and Peter Field as my deputy secretaries.[4] We embarked on a very intensive period when we put the two departments together.

The reason I raise this is because the newspaper I write for recently ran a vigorous campaign asking whether this had been such a good idea after all. It did so in the context of the Australian Wheat Board scandal. Their argument was that if you had kept the two departments separate, the old Department of Foreign Affairs, with its focus on concerns about rigorous enforcement of United Nations Security Council resolutions, would have made certain that this would not have happened. Because it was an amalgamated organisation, so went the argument, it gave priority to trade issues, or at least the same people who were responsible for the foreign policy issues also had to weigh the balance of our trade interests. So rather than having a tremendous contest that would have to be resolved in cabinet, it was resolved at a lower level, even perhaps subconsciously.

I profoundly disagree with that point of view. I always thought that the marriage between Foreign Affairs and Trade was one of the best things that has happened in the public service. It did, at the time, lead to greater application of resources and focus on what were and remain priorities for us — economic and trade issues. But it is a simple fact that, as the counsel assisting the Cole Inquiry into the Australian Wheat Board remarked at the time, in the period up to the middle of 1996 the department had vigorously implemented, overseen and insisted on the letter of the Iraq sanctions. Something changed after that and the investigation was, in part, into what happened.[5]

I think it is fair to say that in my day I never found the government saying to me that I should pull my punches on foreign policy because Australia had an important trade concern at stake. It may have been because of the particular personality of Gareth Evans, the minister at the time, who was such a dominant figure. But I do not think it is a systemic issue and that is the point that I really want to lead into now.

There is a great deal of talk in the press about the independence of the public service — has it been compromised? It was a big issue in my day and indeed there are some people who would say that my very appointment raised this issue. After all, it was no secret that I was a member and a strong supporter of the Labor Party. One is allowed to be such and I think that is still the case. But there could have been a view that I got the job because of my involvement with the ALP.

All I know is that my first job as departmental secretary was as head of the Department of Industrial Relations. We brought in the first enterprise bargaining system in the Australian Public Service, negotiating the first ever federal enterprise bargaining agreement. It was an interesting situation — me and a note-taker on our side of the table and 34 trade unionists on the other.

Leaving aside my appointment, I am worried that somehow there is a view that there is a Platonic ideal of the national interest, which exists somewhere in the ether, that is really only understood by the public service, or indeed in some cases, by the military as, potentially, in Fiji. People who hold this view are saying that we, the public servant and the military, are the final repositories of what is the public interest. Prime Minister Thaksin Shinawatra of Thailand may have been democratically elected and was almost certain to be re-elected overwhelmingly in the next election, but he was seen by the military to be 'acting against the public interest', so he was replaced. You hear the same argument from the commander of the armed forces in Fiji. There seems to be a residual idea that there is a higher loyalty among public servants or the military than to the government of the day. In my view, this is absolutely and completely wrong.

We all have our views of what constitutes the national interest. We can all go to an election and contest it, by standing ourselves, or supporting particular political parties or simply by voting. In the end, the people who are elected in an election are the people who decide, for the period of their time in government, what is going to be the national interest. So, it is the duty of public servants to give the best, firmest and clearest, most uncompromising policy advice they possibly can and, indeed, to press it hard if they believe it. But, it is also their job to accept the answer or, if they cannot tolerate it, to ask to be shifted somewhere else or to leave. I say this because many people to whom I feel close and with whom I identify on policy issues, seem to me to have a view that somehow in accepting a minister's decision a public servant is compromising their independence. In my view, they are not; they are simply doing their job.

This is one of the things that makes me uncomfortable about 'freedom of information'. There has been a lot of argument about this, but it can make you uncomfortable about committing some things to paper as a public servant because, when you say things in very direct terms in writing to a minister, you worry that someone might get access to it and the minister might be politically damaged by quotes from contrary advice from the public service. If for some reason or other the minister gets advice and does not act on it, it is seen as an outrage and a disgrace, yet it is their job as minister to make the decision.

Michael Costello, AO

In a legitimate debate about what should be open and what should not, this is a problem which is not given enough credence, yet I do feel it is having a real impact on what public servants are prepared to put on record in notes and advice.

The absolute key, in my view, was the independence of the secretary and the senior officers. That is why I opposed the legislation of 1984, brought in by Labor, removing the permanency of secretaries. It is why I opposed the introduction of contracts in 1994 and refused to accept one. Secretaries and senior officers of the department are the bulwark, knowing that, while they may be removed from a particular job by a minister, they are not going to be thrown on the scrap heap of unemployment at the age of 45. It was suggested to me that a secretary was cowardly to put their livelihood ahead of the national interest and this may be true. But if you have kids at school and things like that to worry about, you might be tempted.

In the end, whether it is ministerial staff or ministers or whatever, what matters is the culture established by the government of the day. You can have all the systems, checks and balances that you like, but it is the culture established by the minister of that department and, indeed, by the cabinet of the day, that matters. I think the problems you see in the Immigration Department are not systemic, but are undoubtedly the result of the culture established there. I am not saying it is an illegitimate culture — I am not arguing that here, although I have my personal views — but it is a culture established by the government and it bears the responsibility for this.

I will now turn to some big policy issues of the day and focus on one of the issues that distresses me even today and this is trade. During my time as secretary, the Uruguay Round of trade negotiations came to fruition. It was a tremendous time for trade policy: huge advances were made in that round. One of the reasons was because Australia resisted the drive by the United States Secretary of State, James Baker, for what the Americans described as a 'hubs and spokes' policy. That is, the United States would be the hub and they would send out spokes and we would all be little points revolving around the United States. So the United States wanted preferential trade agreements. We resisted this as strongly as we could because we knew it would undermine the Uruguay Round negotiations and we were able to stop it.

One of the tragedies of trade policy today is that we have fallen for these so-called bilateral free trade agreements that are properly called Preferential Trade Agreements. Despite all the arguments to the contrary, I do not think there is any doubt that it has undermined dramatically and drastically the drive for a new round of multilateral trade liberalisation. I think it has substantially undermined support for free trade in the United States in particular, yet US support for a multilateral round is really the *sine qua non*. You will see after the November 2006 mid-term election in the United States a substantial period ahead when the Congress will not support new multilateral free trade arrangements: you might as well put them on the back burner. I put this down primarily to this drive for preferential trade agreements.

I will now turn to Asia. This is a big subject. Many people associate Paul Keating with Australia's push into Asia, but in fact it goes back to the 1950s. It goes back to Dick Woolcott who invented APEC. But it is true to say that both Bob Hawke and especially Keating gave greater emphasis to our involvement in Asia. One of the things that is very unfortunate about the debate in this country is that it was portrayed as a policy of 'we are Asians'. The then Leader of the Opposition, John Howard, claimed that the policy of the Labor Party was to make us Asians and that it was a policy of downgrading the relationship with the United States, which was quite untrue.

Keating's drive at the time was, in significant part, due to his concern about a disengagement of the United States from the region. He believed it would be bad for our national interest if the United States was to lose interest in Asia and to focus only on narrow aspects of its relationship with the Eastern Rim of the Pacific. That was why he worked so hard to take what was originally a Hawke proposal, that is APEC, and to turn it into something much bigger. Dick Woolcott led the effort as the Government's Special Envoy and, later, I had a modest role as secretary.

The aim of APEC was to create an overarching structure that would commit the United States at presidential level to the region, along with China. It worked for a while but, unfortunately, there was a strong drive by Prime Minister Mahathir of Malaysia, strongly but privately supported by China, to enlarge APEC so much that it would lose a lot of its salience. They succeeded substantially in doing this.

The ASEAN Regional Forum, an Evans initiative, was also established at this time. I simply do not know enough to comment on how well it is working now. What we have really seen in the last 10 years is a Chinese effort to create structures that will exclude the United States, which is working pretty well. The East Asian Summit will, over time, challenge the APEC Summit — you will not get heads of countries coming to two leadership meetings on a regular basis — and of course the key thing about the East Asian Summit is that it does not include the United States. This is not just the fault of the Chinese and those who planned it this way. It is also the fault of the United States which in this presidential period has had far less interest in the structures of South East Asia, focusing instead on North Asia as it traditionally did: first, the threat from China and, now, from North Korea plus the relationship with Japan. It is much less interested in the broader sweep of events in the region. This represents a backward step.

Michael Costello, AO

On the subject of Australia's relations with Indonesia, we live with deep distrust between the two countries, not just from our side, but from their side towards us. Probably, in Australia it is a sentiment that is found in our population. In Indonesia, it is partly population, but their elites are more hostile and dislike us far more than our elites dislike and distrust Indonesia. This results from Australian governments doing things that were unavoidable, such as in East Timor and taking refugees from West Irian (West Papua, as it is called now). It is very hard to convince Indonesia, despite the new Australian security agreement with them, that Australians do not secretly support the separation of West Papua.

Why is that? Because we once had an absolutely adamant, uncompromising commitment to Indonesia's sovereignty in East Timor. Indeed, Prime Minister Howard's famous letter to then President B.J. Habibie proposing the great referendum said the whole purpose of this was to support the Government's absolute commitment to the continued incorporation of East Timor into Indonesia. Unfortunately, Habibie was one of the more erratic human beings and went down a path that was entirely unexpected.

But imagine your feelings about this if you were an Indonesian. You had seen Australian political parties on both sides (and Prime Minister Howard more vigorously than perhaps any other figure, if you go back and read his statements over 20 years) saying that East Timor is part of Indonesia and we will continue to support that when, in the end, we did not. What would you, as an Indonesian, think when we make similar protestations about Irian Jaya? So we have a really difficult time ahead of us that is not going to be solved by one prime minister or a particular government. It will take perhaps 50 years of sustained effort and I do not think we are putting the sustained effort into the human and cultural language links that we need.

As for 'the Great Powers', I remember it being said in the 1980s that Japan was going to take over the world and be the world's number one economy. Some said this meant the end of the American empire. Whoops! In the 1990s there was the collapse of the Soviet Union and the end of the East-West conflict — at least it seemed that way. The United States was the sole superpower: described by Bill Clinton's Secretary of State as the 'indispensable superpower', described today as the 'unavoidable superpower'. Now, of course, we are seeing the limits of that power.

We are seeing the rise of China and India, particularly economically. This is hardly surprising, even looking back to the evidence available then. If you pour in enough labour and enough capital then, as the Soviet Union found right up to the mid-1960s, your economy can grow faster than anyone else's. But there is a certain point where you hit technology barriers where you cannot pour in any more labour and capital: you need much higher levels of technology and skills and training. China and India are nowhere near that point yet, but China is probably nearer to it than India.

In my view the Western Alliance — and this is a big statement — is fairly much dead. On Islam: we missed its rise; we missed the implications of the return of Khomeini and the hostage crisis in Iran; we missed the implications of Hezbollah; we missed the implications of what was happening with the various terrorist attacks of the time. We simply did not grasp its fundamental importance to the next 20 or 30 years. I think we still underestimate how important and how fundamental this is going to be for us.

The main problem for Australia remains much the same. We do not have the military power to impose our will on others. The Solomon Islands and Papua New Guinea — even East Timor — have shown us that. We do not have the economic power to bribe others to get our way. We need to persuade people. It is a very old fashioned idea and it is called diplomacy. We need to invest a huge amount of time, effort and resources into it.

One of the things I did when I was secretary was have a global plan approved by the cabinet for a substantial increase in the resources we devoted to the Department of Foreign Affairs and Trade on the political side, rather than just trade. I felt we really needed to up upgrade our political reporting on Indonesia, the region and the world. It was great plan, but there was a change of government and the department was cut by 25 per cent for budgetary reasons and it was not possible. I think this argument remains valid and I think it is particularly true in the case of Indonesia. Dick Woolcott coined a phrase: Australia is 'the odd man in of Asia'. That means 'yes', we are part of it; 'yes', we do our best; but always as the slightly odd figure at the table. We have got to learn to be comfortable with that and operate that way, rather than insisting we can be just like the other Asians. We are not like them and they do not think we are and, indeed, our own people do not think we are.

What about the 'realism' versus 'idealism' debate? What it comes down to is this: I always like to have in my mind the three 'Ps' — principle, pragmatism and patience. I believe if you do not have, at the forefront of your foreign policy and the way you conduct it, the right principles — that is ideals — you will fail in the medium to long term. I do not believe the idea that stability, above all, is the key idea. I think that has been disproved. But you need absolute pragmatism in pursuit of those principles and ideals and that is exactly what we have not seen in the case of the current war in Iraq. No pragmatism, no quality in execution, no ability to undertake this properly and think it through carefully and to accept that it might take 15 to 25 years to achieve your goals there and that you will then have to take steps sideways and backwards. You cannot achieve it in five minutes. It is not a 'McDonald's' world when it comes to foreign policy.

This brings me to the third point — patience. When I look back at our success with Cambodia, we did something that was well worthwhile.³ But you would not look at Cambodia now and say how wonderful it is, because it isn't and it won't be for maybe another 30 years. The Western world's own attainment of democracy, liberalism and economic success took us centuries and we should not expect that we can achieve these ideals quickly there. But what we must not do is take those issues off the agenda.

The task remains the same and the principles remain the same. The quality of the people working in the department is as high, if not higher than it ever was. They are outstanding individuals. I do not know the current secretary but, by all accounts, he is a fine person. You look at people like Nick Warner in Defence, which is a fine appointment. Ric Smith was a great leader, Dennis Richardson, Paul O'Sullivan, all first rate people.⁶

So in the end we can fall into the danger of focusing too much on 'it is not the way it was in our day'. No, it is not; it is a different game. But in the end, the whole culture, the whole approach, is set by the government of the day. That is, what we as public servants and diplomats have to accept. That is the key conclusion I have come to looking back on that time. The quality of the politicians and their ideology is what dictates how you proceed.

Question: The rise of China is a major challenge. How do we go about adjusting to it?

The reality of Chinese power is that it is not as great as many think it is. The Chinese economy is still quite a bit smaller than that of California and its military capability — its strategic reach — is extremely limited. However, in military and security terms, where it matters is dragging in our allies into a conflict over Taiwan. This is the only circumstance where I could see China using military power outside its borders, unless something truly unexpected happens in Korea.

My view of China is that they regard the last 400 to 500 years as an aberration. They see, along with parts of the Islamic world, that the time of the West is over and they will return to their rightful position as the leading power in the world sometime in the next 40 or 50 years. I think they are also very patient about it. They have that pragmatism and patience I was talking about and they are going to risk little in achieving their goals. They are certainly going to risk very little within their country. There is no particular sign of any liberalisation. Our problem is that we are dealing with a country that is a dictatorship and, quite often a particularly unpleasant one. Yet we have important economic and trade interests with it.

We have managed this before and I do not see that we should not continue to be able to do so. But what worries me is if we pursue fundamental human rights issues with China only in a purely pro forma way. I think you can do both because, in the end, China is pragmatic. If it needs what we have to sell, it will buy it at the right price. So you can pursue human rights in a real way. But China is obsessed — and I can see why — with easing the United States out of this part of the world. I think the Americans have relatively little interest in South-east Asia and that is a factor in the present US government's total preoccupation with the Middle East and North Asia. We are going to be more on our own and whether or not Australia can be in lock-step with the United States in this part of the world is a big question.

I do not think that simply saying 'have whatever you want' is a basis for policy towards China any more than it should be a policy in relation to any other country. But I fear there is a strong lobby in Australia, particularly in the business community, which feels this should be the case.

Question: There seems to be a push to put some substance into our relations with India. This has happened at least four times. Have we left it too late?

I think we have tried. You can only court someone if they want to be courted. They simply were not interested in us, in part for a good long while because they saw us as simply lackeys of the Americans and their tilt was towards the Soviet Union. I remember trying to engage the Indians myself as part of one of those efforts you have recalled. It was one of my many failures — they just were not interested. They visited Australia; we had what we thought were some terrific days; we thought we had broken through the barriers. Then the word came back later to the effect that they had looked at all the ideas we discussed and on reflection decided 'perhaps not'.

I do not think we have missed the boat in economic or trade terms. Who knows? You have in China a disciplined government of a traditional authoritarian kind and it has the curious combination of authoritarian goal-setting but also semi-market forces, at least in the international exposure of its economy. But if you look carefully at what they are doing, you see that they have massive amounts of surplus labour available and they are able to get access to large amounts of capital through their own domestic savings and through foreign investment. If you put the two together and just keep pouring it in, your economy is going to grow and grow strongly.

It happened to the Soviet Union in the 1950s and early 1960s when they were growing more strongly than the United States. When Nikita Khrushchev banged his shoe on the table and said 'we will bury you', he was actually talking about burying the United States economically. And at the time it seemed as though they would. Then they ran out of surplus labour and ran out of capital and they had a technology issue with lack of access to the latest in thinking and ideas.

Michael Costello, AO

I do not think India will face that problem. They are hugely well educated and are involved with some of the world's great institutions. However, I think the Chinese have learnt that lesson too and they are investing hugely in education, which is a challenge to us. One of our most important industries in this country is our education industry. But if we do not invest more in it, through either the public or private sector, much more than we do at the moment, we are not going to be able to attract them and they are going to turn more and more to their own capabilities.

To sum up, we are far from too late with India. If the Indians see there is a dollar to be made from us, they will be in it. If we are not worth trading with, they won't. We just have to be competitive.

Question: Cambodia was a success, can you comment on the drivers that made it a success and their application to the problems of today?

The negotiations were a success. But everyone focuses on that extremely brief period from late 1989 to the middle of 1990. The deal was actually done in September 1990. But the process began in 1983. Bill Hayden worked very hard at it for three or four years, but it did not work then, the reason being the geo-strategic situation did not allow it. At the time the Soviet Union was still a dominant power, second only to the United States: China saw itself as being threatened by the Russians on its northern border and on its southern border it saw itself as being threatened by Vietnam, a Soviet ally as it was then. It saw Cambodia as a field for playing out that conflict, so it gave its support to the Khmer Rouge.

When that changed and the Soviet Union collapsed, Moscow could no longer afford to have Vietnam as a client and Vietnam said, 'we are sorry, we cannot be in Cambodia any more'. The Chinese saw that they did not have to worry about Vietnam being a threat. It also meant that the Thais no longer had the threat of the Vietnamese against their border. So the whole geo-strategic situation opened up and the reason Australia had credibility to pull this off was because of Hayden. By that time the Prime Minister of Cambodia was Hun Sen and he had been Foreign Minister beforehand. Hayden had met him in Ho Chi Minh City, but the Hayden initiative ended because the whole of ASEAN objected, regarding this as an act of total treachery. But Hun Sen remembered it and regarded it as an act of great courage. So did Vietnam.

So we dreamt up this idea of a United Nations role. It was the change in the Big Power relationships that made possible what was simply not possible before. You can only do things that geo-strategic reality will allow you to do. Just having good ideas and being energetic and vigorous will not make it happen. Yet, equally, if it had not been for that meeting between Hayden and Hun Sen in Ho

Chi Minh City we would have had no standing. We would have been seen as another lackey of the United States. That is how most of the region saw us and, to a certain extent, still do. It is a fact that whatever political party is in office in Australia we are going to be a close ally of the United States. That is how people think about us. Sometimes that is very useful.

Question: Do you think we underestimate American awareness of Asia?

Popular American awareness of South-east Asia is about zero, but then it is about zero for the rest of the world. There are people in the United States who are experts on this part of the world but the United States made no effort to be part of the East Asia Summit and said to us, 'go ahead and join'. In 1989 James Baker was outraged when Hawke first proposed APEC and the United States was not supposed to be in it. I was at the meeting between Gareth Evans and Jim Baker when this came up and it was a terrible meeting. But now — I do not think it is good or bad — the Americans have just got other focuses: the Middle East, North Asia and Japan. I just think other things are more to the forefront in their minds and it is a lot harder than it was to get their attention.

That should not alarm us. But I am concerned about this perception that Australia is a 'poodle' of the United States. (I always think these epithets are extremely unhelpful.) The Coalition parties and the Labor Party do have different approaches, but the sort of thing that Howard was saying about Labor trashing the relationship with the United States and giving it a low priority, is completely wrong. It is also completely wrong for people to say we are behaving like a poodle by deciding to be close to the United States. We are not.

The Howard Government, quite early in its life, made a calculated decision about our national interest that the right thing to do would be to be as close as we possibly could to the United States, the world's number one economic and military power, and that was the smart thing to do. Whether it was or it wasn't, I do not think they felt like poodles. You might remember that George Bush was not in office when that decision was made and Bill Clinton was never particularly nice to John Howard.

So I think these ways of characterising policy towards the United States do not help very much. People have different views, but there is one coherent view and that is no matter which political party you are in, with the possible exception of the Greens, there is a strong commitment to the United States relationship. The difference may be that there is a much greater willingness on the part of Labor to have disagreements with them.

The Labor Party is always going to feel more comfortable with a Democratic president and a Republican government in the United States will feel happier with a Coalition Government here. They have common political interests and common domestic policies in many cases. I do not see why people should see this as a strange thing. Labor had a perfectly decent relationship with Reagan and Jim Baker, but there was a much closer relationship with Clinton. This [the Howard] Government had a perfectly respectable relationship with Clinton as far as I am aware, but has a very close relationship with its political soul-mate, the Republican Party.

Conclusion: Idealism and pragmatism

I went to a Lowy Institute seminar which, from left, right and centre, was basically a 'Bag Bush' fest over Iraq. The most common theme was how naïve, innocent and foolish the Americans were to have this ideal of supporting liberty around the world: that this could not be a basis for foreign policy; and that in this world you had to be realistic and promote stability as the key.

Of all people, Robert Manne[7] gave a lecture on the importance of the Treaty of Westphalia which established the principle of national sovereignty. I recall that the Soviet Union used to quote the Treaty of Westphalia to me when we used to raise human rights issues with them. Every crummy dictator around the world used to give us lectures about the principles of mutual respect, sovereignty, independence and non-interference in internal affairs, the codeword being 'let us murder our people without you saying anything'. I was not particularly persuaded by that argument.

The other idea that was repeatedly referred to was 'containment'. Couldn't we have contained Iraq as we had done successfully with the Soviet Union, went the argument. Some success — sanctions in Iraq were supposed to contain Iraq, but became a complete shambles as the Chinese, Russians and especially the French, cheated on them as fast as they could go. What I had not realised is that an Australian company was a big cheater too.

People kept quoting the case of the Soviet Union, which they said had been successfully contained for more than 40 years after World War II, without the risks we were taking with Iraq. But part of the policy of containment of the Soviet Union were doctrines called 'mutually assured destruction' and 'extended deterrence'. Under the principles of containment, it was policy that if the Soviet Union attacked the United States or Western Europe, or us, or Japan, by conventional means, the United States would respond with a nuclear attack which would undoubtedly bring a nuclear attack on the United States and the rest of us.

It seems to me that this was far less realist, far less cautious or pragmatic and non-idealistic than anything Bush has ever proposed. Huge risks were taken in the name of containment, not only in the early 1960s, but in early 1983 when, during Exercise Archer in Western Europe, the Soviets misread all the signals and thought the Americans and Western Europeans were about to launch an attack on them. So every time I hear that containment was such a moderate, cautious, sensible policy in pursuit of a great principle — we were not going to let Western Europe be taken over; we were not going to let the Soviet Union run large parts of the world — I am reminded that huge risks were taken which, fortunately, for us all never eventuated.

The pursuit of stability has been a highly sterile policy. It was stability that led us to support Iraq against Iran.

You have got to have clear ideals — and just because George Bush said it, does not mean it is not true. His second inaugural address was one of the great modern speeches you will read. But nobody took any notice of it because it was viewed through the prism of 'pre-emption', Iraq, aggressive cowboy-style language, language he has the good sense now to regret that he used. If you go back and read it now, it was fantastic — great ideals, full of humility, but by that time it was too late. Bush had lost that battle.

ENDNOTES

[1] Huntington's article later appeared as a book *The Clash of Civilizations and the Remaking of World Order*, New York: Simon & Schuster, 1996.

[2] *Seeking Asian Engagement: Australia in World Affairs 1991-95*, edited by James Cotton and John Ravenhill, Oxford University Press, Australia, Melbourne, 1997.

[3] Paul Kelly, 'The Cunningham Lecture for the Australian Academy of Social Sciences', Occasional Paper Series 4/2005.

[4] Peter Field and Mike Lightowler were deputy secretaries in the Department of Trade at the time of the amalgamation of the Foreign Affairs and Trade in 1987. Deputy secretary from 1987–94, Peter Field was Australia's Chief Negotiator for the Uruguay Round of Multilateral Trade Negotiations.

[5] See Linda Botterill 'Doing it for the Growers in Iraq?: The AWB, Oil-for-Food and the Cole Inquiry', *Australian Journal of Public Administration*, Volume 66, Issue 1, pp. 4-12, March 2007.

[6] Ric Smith was Secretary of Defence (2002-06), Dennis Richardson was Director-General of the Australian Security Intelligence Organisation (ASIO) (1996-2005), and Paul O'Sullivan succeeded him in 2005.

[7] Robert Manne is Professor of Politics at La Trobe University in Melbourne and was for many years editor of *Quadrant*, the 'independent' journal of 'ideas and literature'.

Philip Flood, AO

Secretary, Department of Foreign Affairs and Trade, 1996–99

Background

The advent of the Howard Government in March 1996 was very significant in foreign policy terms because foreign policy was seen as one of the issues that led to the defeat of the Keating Labor Government. Howard, with Alexander Downer as his Foreign Minister, brought significant changes to the priorities and conduct of Australian policy.

Philip Flood was appointed as secretary by the Howard Government at the beginning of its term of office. He had already had a distinguished career serving governments of both political persuasions in high-level positions, including as director-general of the Office of National Assessments (ONA) (1995–96), director-general of the Australian Agency for International Development (AusAID) (1993–95) and chief executive officer for Special Trade Representations (1977–80). He was also Ambassador to Indonesia (1989–93).

During Flood's secretaryship, the first challenge was to respond to the Howard Government's determination to differentiate itself from the foreign policy of its Australian Labor Party predecessors. In Flood's term he was involved in preparation of Australia's first ever *White Paper* on Foreign and Trade Policy, which was notable for confirming the government's strong preference for bilateralism over regionalism and multilateralism. A further early challenge was dealing with the 1997 Asian financial crisis that transformed the region in favour of China and eventually terminated the Soeharto regime in Indonesia.

Australia's alliance with the United States would reach new levels of intimacy and policy convergence. While this reflected Howard's strong conviction that the United States would be more, not less, important to Australia, it also occurred partly through coincidence of events as much as planning. In time, the Howard Government would also attach high priority to engagement with Australia's broader Asia Pacific region; his government would prove highly pro-active in its nearer region of the South Pacific and East Timor and would bring Australia into a closer relationship with China.

One of the more serious managerial tasks for DFAT at this time was dealing with the reductions in the departmental budget and, therefore, staff numbers, directed by the new government. Despite this challenge, Flood secured strong staff support for far-reaching changes to employment conditions, bringing much greater flexibility to the management of the Department. A significant event was the Department's move into new premises designed to meet the special needs of a foreign ministry, the first time this had been done.

After his term as secretary, Philip Flood was appointed High Commissioner to the United Kingdom. Subsequently, he conducted several public inquiries for the Australian Government, including a sensitive inquiry into Australia's Intelligence Agencies in 2004.

Flood Presentation: 23 November 2006

Cardinal de Richelieu (Armand Jean du Plessis), the French statesman and cleric, formed the first distinct foreign ministry in 1626. Since France dominated European power politics in the century after Richelieu's death, France's system of foreign policy organisation was gradually emulated by other states. Richelieu's confidant, the Capuchin friar Père Joseph (born François Le Clerc du Tremblay), was the diplomat used by the Cardinal in all of the most difficult negotiations of a critical period that included the Thirty Years' War. Because of the colour of his habit, Le Clerc became known as the éminence grise and this term was subsequently used to describe any unelected power behind a throne.

Papua New Guinea applied the term to me on 19 March 1997. I had been asked by Australia's Prime Minister to be his emissary in negotiating with Papua New Guinea's Prime Minister the removal of mercenaries from his country's territory. The handling of this issue, and its outcome, highlighted an important shift in the Australian Government's approach to foreign policy.

On 18 February 1997, the Office of National Assessments had briefed the Prime Minister and other ministers on the basis of intelligence that the PNG Government had signed a $36 million contract with a British-based private military consultancy firm, Sandline International. In entering into this contract — which was for the supply of arms, training and mercenaries — the PNG Government had the dual objectives of destroying the Bougainville Revolutionary Army and reopening the Panguna copper mine on Bougainville. For a long time an intractable rebellion had been underway there, forcing the closure of the mine and causing extensive death and suffering.

For Australia, this represented a major foreign policy issue, for several reasons:

- mercenaries were being brought into Australia's sphere of influence;
- there was considerable risk that the arrangements between the PNG government and Sandline would bring great instability to our closest neighbour which, at that time, was receiving over $300 million in civil aid, as well as substantial defence assistance; and
- many of the up to 10,000 Australian citizens living in PNG would be at risk if there were to be a breakdown in law and order.

In response to the ONA briefing, the Prime Minister summoned several ministers and senior officials — members of the National Security Committee of Cabinet — and the lines of Australian policy were determined. Broadly speaking, they were:

- we should aim to stop the mercenaries, then training in Wewak, from deploying to Bougainville;
- we should then get the mercenaries out of Papua New Guinea;
- the Australian Defence Force should look at options for assisting in this operation; and
- we should try to achieve our objectives in such a way as to do the least damage to relations with Papua New Guinea.

The Prime Minister spoke by telephone to PNG's Prime Minister, Sir Julius Chan. Sir Julius was less than frank about his plans. However, as it happened, there was to be another opportunity for Australia to sound him out on Sandline's activities. Australia's Foreign Minister, Alexander Downer, was due in Port Moresby on 19 February — the day following the ONA briefing — and while there he was able to meet face to face with Sir Julius. The essence of his advice to Downer was that what was taking place in Wewak was no more than the training of the PNG armed forces.

The two Prime Ministers subsequently met at Kirribilli House, the Prime Minister's official residence in Sydney. Again there was no movement in regard to the substance of the issues that were of concern to Australia.

On Monday 17 March the crisis deepened when, in defiance of his Prime Minister, Brigadier General Jerry Singirok, Commander of the Papua New Guinea Defence Force, launched an operation — codenamed 'Rausim Kwik' — to remove Sandline from PNG. Singirok ordered the arrest of Tim Spicer, the Sandline chief in PNG, and then provoked a constitutional crisis by demanding the resignation of his country's Prime Minister, Deputy Prime Minister and Defence Minister.

Sir Julius Chan sacked Singirok that same afternoon and appointed an interim Commander of the Papua New Guinea Defence Force. Singirok refused to budge and unrest spread in Port Moresby. The Government's response divided the army. The police, however, supported the Prime Minister.

On Tuesday 18 March, after consulting the National Security Committee, Prime Minister Howard told Parliament that:

- Australia supported the elected government of Papua New Guinea (i.e. we did not support Singirok's demands for the resignation of ministers);
- Australia remained opposed to PNG's use of mercenaries; and
- the Australian Government was concerned for the welfare of Australian citizens at risk of being caught up in the civil unrest.

On Wednesday 19 March, following further consultations with the National Security Committee, the Prime Minister telephoned Sir Julius Chan and told him that the sacking of Singirok had Australia's support. Howard also asked him if he would receive me as his personal emissary. Sir Julius, who knew me from previous negotiations I had conducted with him over aid to PNG, agreed. That same afternoon, I left for Port Moresby in the Australian Government's VIP Falcon jet. I was accompanied by Hugh White, deputy secretary of the Department of Defence, and Allan Taylor, then with the Prime Minister's Department.[1] Allan Taylor is an outstanding diplomat and Hugh White is Australia's foremost authority on defence and strategic policy. When in the air, Hugh prudently observed that we could not be sure we would be able to land should troops loyal to Singirok choose to intervene. Fortunately, this proved not to be a problem.

I met Sir Julius the next morning, in his office on the fourth floor of PNG's Parliament House. Australia's High Commissioner, David Irvine, joined my colleagues and me. Sir Julius was accompanied by the head of his department, Noel Levi. Sir Julius had contributed much to PNG and this was his second term as Prime Minister. He had also been PNG's first Finance Minister following independence. An arresting-looking man, with features drawn from his Chinese father and New Ireland mother, Chan was a strong nationalist. Hardworking and competent, he was also autocratic and aloof.

I told Sir Julius that, if he did not abandon the idea of using mercenaries, Australia would take drastic action and that it would affect both the aid program and the Defence Cooperation Program. He was taken aback. He was then offered additional assistance if he walked away from the Sandline deal. Eventually he tried to bargain. 'Perhaps Australia might like to pay for the mercenaries?' I said no. There was a total deadlock. The meeting broke up after some hours and I returned to our hotel. That evening Sir Julius's office telephoned to advise that he was reviewing his position and would see me in the morning.

On Friday 21 March he told me that he was suspending the Sandline contract while he set up a judicial inquiry and, most importantly, that the Sandline mercenaries would start leaving PNG that afternoon. My party flew out of Port Moresby later that day. Mr Howard met us in Sydney and he announced the outcome. The events surrounding the Sandline affair led to Sir Julius Chan's resignation on 26 March and the end of his political career.

The immediate outcomes of our negotiations were:

- (of course) the withdrawal of the mercenaries from PNG;
- the upholding of the integrity of the PNG constitution (in other words, the military commander Jerry Singirok neither determined the civilian government nor took control himself); and

- the opening up of new opportunities to address the problems in Bougainville.

The Howard Government's approach to this crisis marked a departure in Australia's South Pacific policy — breaking the mould in terms of official forbearance towards PNG and demonstrating a willingness to be more proactive in the region. The resolution of the crisis demonstrated Australia's capacity to bring considerable leverage to bear in regional diplomacy.

The handling of the events of early 1997 also demonstrated the importance of the National Security Committee (NSC) in the Government's approach to foreign, defence and security policy. Like Hawke, but unlike Whitlam, Keating, Blair or Bush, Howard is a cabinet traditionalist who cares strongly about orderly cabinet process. Accordingly, the NSC, which John Howard has called 'one of the very significant successes of the Government in terms of governance arrangements', is a key cabinet function under the Howard Government. The NSC has also given the Prime Minister a strong grip on the details of foreign, defence and security policy and, under Howard, has had a broader agenda than any comparable committee used by any of his predecessors.

I had the privilege of being secretary of the Department of Foreign Affairs and Trade at the time of a new government with different ideas about foreign and trade policy. Changes of government have occurred on only four occasions in the past 50 years. Other secretaries who had the experience of guiding the Department as it adjusted to a new government were Sir Keith Waller in 1972, Alan Renouf in 1975 and Peter Henderson in 1983.

In a broad sense Howard and Downer came to government with an assessment of Australia's place in the international community that was similar to the perspective of the Hawke and Keating governments. All held an optimistic view of Australia as a leading middle power with the capacity to influence events. All believed that Australia — while of course lacking the strength upon which a great power can draw in order to impose its will — is large enough and clever enough to advance specific interests in key areas.

But beyond this similarity, much about foreign and trade policy changed with the advent of the new government. Howard and Downer changed substantially the direction of Australia's foreign and strategic policy. They brought to government a very different perspective on major power relations, a different view of Australia's relationship with the United States, a different perception of other major bilateral relations, a different approach to trade and to the environment, and a different assessment of what the United Nations and other multilateral institutions should be tasked to achieve.

John Howard brought, in particular, a more expansive and optimistic view of the influence of the United States and a conviction that the United States and Australia are destined to grow more important to each other. He wanted strong links with Japan, China and Indonesia but he would never use Keating's narrow, if confident, construction, 'Australia must find its security in Asia, not from Asia'.[2] Howard came to office respectful of Indonesia but less enamoured than Keating became with Indonesia's President Suharto. A passionate believer in parliamentary democracy and the rule of law, Howard was always going to have more reservations about Suharto. In a conversation shortly after his election, and following a successful first meeting with Malaysia's Prime Minster, Dr Mahathir, the Prime Minister discussed with me his approach to foreign leaders. He remarked: 'We are proud to be Australian, proud of our culture and traditions — we do not grovel to foreign leaders. I will be defiantly Australian without being gauche or provocative.'

One of Alexander Downer's early decisions was to issue the *White Paper on Foreign and Trade Policy*.[3] I would like to say that this was done on my recommendation, but it was not. Downer personally took this initiative and, at the time, I reflected how strange it was that his two energetic and capable predecessors — Hayden and Evans — had not done so. Downer set up an advisory committee, consisting of business people, a former Prime Minister, former policy advisers and academics to give him additional advice.

One of the best decisions I made was to agree to the request of Peter Varghese, the present Director-General of ONA, that he be in charge of the secretariat charged with drafting the text of the *White Paper*. Downer drove the process personally and, given the closeness between his strategic vision and that of the Prime Minister, it was not a difficult matter for the Foreign Minister to secure cabinet endorsement for his text.

The *White Paper* acknowledged elements of continuity between governments and noted 'the priority accorded to the Asia Pacific and, especially, to the countries of East Asia, the forging of close relationships with the United States, Japan, Indonesia and China, the commitment to further trade liberalisation and strong support for the World Trade Organisation and APEC'.[4] The document further set out four strategic priorities:

- The Government will apply a basic national interest test to its foreign and trade policy: does it advance the security, jobs and standard of living of Australians?
- Australia has global interests that require an active foreign and trade policy, of broad scope. In terms of this policy, the Asia Pacific is the highest priority.
- Bilateral relationships will be the principal means of advancing Australia's interests, and will be the basic building blocks for effective regional and global strategies.

- Australia will adopt a more selective approach to multilateral issues and must concentrate its multilateral efforts in those areas where Australia's security and economic interests are closely engaged.

The following brief extracts from the *White Paper* give a sense of its flavour:

- Australia's foreign and trade policy is about advancing the interests of Australia and Australians ...
- The United States will remain, over the next 15 years, the single most powerful country in the world. The Government's judgment is that the United States will also continue to see its best interests being served by maintaining its strategic engagement in East Asia ... The strategic engagement and commitment [of the United States] underwrites the stability of East Asia ...
- China's economic growth, with attendant confidence and enhanced influence, will be the most important strategic development of the next 15 years. How China manages its economic growth and pursues its international objectives, and how other nations, particularly the United States and Japan, respond to China will be crucial ...
- Australia's strong links to Europe and the United States ... enhance Australia's value to East Asia ... Australia does not need to choose between its history and its geography ...
- Australia must be realistic about what multilateral institutions such as the United Nations system can deliver ...
- Central to the strategies in this paper is adopting a whole-of-nation approach which emphasises the linkages between domestic policies and foreign and trade policies.

Behind the words in the *White Paper* were many nuances of difference with the previous government. One of the document's underlying messages was that Australia should be proud of its unique identity and that our neighbours should value us for what we are: a responsible, constructive and practical nation with remarkable achievements in medicine, agriculture, mining, education, law and, not least, in governance and public administration.

Howard and Downer had a more positive view than their predecessors with regard to Australia's relationship with Britain. This was no yearning for an Anglo-Celtic past. Neither had any illusions that Britain would stand up within the European Community when issues with the potential to affect Australia's agricultural interests arose, but both had greater respect than Keating for what Britain represented and what it could bring to the international table. Both also valued highly Australia's military and intelligence links with Britain.

Similarly, Downer had no illusions about France's capacity to play an idiosyncratic role in global affairs but he was much more convinced than his predecessors had been about the importance of keeping France — indeed Europe — engaged in the South Pacific. He shared with Paul Keating an affection for French culture, but drew different conclusions about France's approach to its territories in the Pacific.

On China, the *White Paper* sent a clear message to Australians: they should understand that China will be a powerful force in our region and a powerful factor affecting the fortunes of Australia. The policy rejected the 'China threat' view, which had taken hold in some influential quarters in the United States. Americans had been debating, and still debate, whether the United States should see China as a strategic competitor or a strategic partner.

In its very early months the Howard Government took a less nuanced approach to China. Responding to a temporary crisis over the Taiwan Straits, Australia gave prompt and strong diplomatic support for American naval manoeuvres intended to reassure Taiwan. In July 1996 the 'Sydney Statement' was issued following the Australia-United States ministerial talks (AUSMIN). China wrongly interpreted this statement as a manifestation of Australian involvement in a US policy of containment. A change in each country's perception began when the Prime Minister met China's President, Jiang Zemin, at the APEC forum in November that year, and both agreed to exchange head of government visits.

Prime Minister Howard's first visit to China, in March 1997, marked a major turning point in his approach to Sino-Australian relations. I had been asked to go ahead and clear the way for a changed approach on several issues. Howard's visit was an outstanding success and laid the foundation for a more strategic relationship and for subsequent commercial achievements.

In addition to its positions in respect of specific bilateral relationships, the *White Paper* gave priority to reforming the treaty making process so as to provide for greater transparency and accountability. Downer also had new ideas about foreign aid policy and he set about changing Australia's aid program. He had strong views about consular matters as well. On my first day as secretary he made it clear that he wanted consular matters to have a higher standing in the department and he wished to be personally involved in any significant consular issue.

On the issue of race, the *White Paper* delivered a strong, principled and unambiguous statement:

> Central to the values to which the Government gives expression is an unqualified commitment to racial equality and to eliminating racial discrimination ... The rejection of racial discrimination is not only a moral issue, it is fundamental to our acceptance by, and engagement with, the region where our vital security and economic interests lie.

> Racial discrimination is not only morally repugnant, it repudiates Australia's best interests.

The issue of race had become a substantive problem for the Foreign Affairs and Trade portfolio because of statements made by the newly elected member of parliament, Pauline Hanson. On 10 September 1996 she had told the Parliament that 'Australia is in danger of being swamped by Asians …' Hanson revived a false image of Australia as a nation opposed to Asian immigration and to strong links with Asia. She also had a warped idea of evidence. She coined the term 'book facts' for the evidence that could be found in books. When challenged to support her assertion that one million illegal immigrants were entering Australia each year, via New Zealand, she replied: 'But you are just asking for "book facts". We don't need "book facts": we know it is happening'. I found her statements on race offensive and, much more importantly, so did Alexander Downer and Tim Fischer, the Minister for Trade. Both portfolio ministers spoke out courageously against Pauline Hanson's views.

The racial aspect of Hanson's speeches was doing Australia damage in a number of Asian capitals and I had several lengthy disagreements with the Prime Minister's office. The Prime Minister had broader political concerns on other issues and these influenced his handling of Hanson. On 8 May 1997, eight months after Hanson's offensive speech in the Parliament, he included an excellent statement on race in the speech he made at a dinner in Sydney to launch the Australian Centre of the Asia Society. He said:

> She cannot have it both ways. She enjoys freedom to express her views. Equally, she has to be accountable for those views. She cannot evade responsibility for the consequences of her statements … She is wrong when she says that Australia is being swamped by Asians. She is wrong to seek scapegoats for society's problems. She is wrong when she denigrates foreign investment, because its withdrawal would cost Australian jobs. She is wrong when she says Australia is headed for civil war.

At the dinner the Prime Minister's Chief of Staff, Grahame Morris, came across to me immediately after the speech and said, 'Are you satisfied now, Philip?', I replied that the Prime Minister's statement was admirable but that — from a foreign policy perspective — it was several months too late.

On trade policy, the new Government was highly committed to APEC and to continuing multilateral reform, but placed more emphasis on bilateral negotiations. The Minister for Trade, Tim Fischer, similarly placed a greater emphasis on bilateral trade marketing.

The integration of Trade functions within a combined Foreign Affairs and Trade portfolio had been a decision of the Hawke Government in 1987. The shift reflected the greater integration of political and economic activities internationally, the growing priority accorded economic issues with the passing of the intensity of the Cold War and continually evolving linkages between domestic and foreign policies. The merging of the two departments also reflected a more strategic approach to public administration.

As Minister for Trade, Tim Fischer introduced an annual Trade Outcomes and Objectives Statement. This was a vehicle for monitoring the effects of efforts to open up markets and for ensuring that trade policy and promotion efforts adequately responded to changing circumstances.

The most important issue the Howard Government had to deal with after those addressed by the White Paper was the collapse of South-East Asian economies. The crisis began on 2 July 1997, when the Thai Government floated the baht. This course of action followed months of pressure from speculators and was undertaken only after the Thai Government had drained the entire reserves of the country's central bank in a futile effort to defend the currency. Then, like a virus, the contagion spread to neighbouring economies — the pressures associated with growth had become too great for the institutional structures of these countries to cope with. Within a year the economies of the countries most affected — Thailand, Indonesia, the Republic of Korea and the Philippines — had shrunk by 18 per cent. Millions of people were plunged back into poverty.

Australia responded generously. Australia and Japan were the only countries to contribute to all three bail-out plans (for Thailand, Indonesia and Korea) by the International Monetary Fund (IMF) with Alexander Downer also playing a critical role in softening the IMF's approach to Indonesia. This involved a blunt showdown between Downer and the US Treasury. And the fact that Australia weathered the crisis influenced the way in which South-East Asia and other regions looked at this country.

As a young Departmental officer having returned from my first posting, I had the privilege of serving for two years as Executive Assistant to the then secretary of the Department, Sir Arthur Tange. Like many others, I admired Tange's intellect, integrity and work ethic, his sense of fairness, his forthright manner and his belief in a distinctively Australian approach to foreign policy and diplomacy. He wanted a department that was vigorous and creative in serving the government of the day. During the time I worked for him, Tange served two ministers: Sir Garfield Barwick and then Paul Hasluck. Both were highly intelligent, hardworking and dedicated to advancing Australia's interests as they saw them. Their differences were instructive.

Garfield Barwick was frank and open with Tange, courteous and trusting, relishing open debate and quickly coming to clear conclusions on the issues at hand. Both minister and secretary understood fully the other's role and prerogatives. Tange was never involved in party politics but he made it his business to understand thoroughly the wider parliamentary and domestic political context in which Barwick had to function. Tange was never subservient and he had the confidence to argue forcefully against what he saw as poor policy.

Paul Hasluck was a fine historian and poet and was widely read. But, in contrast to Barwick, Hasluck could be suspicious, querulous, frequently remote, sometimes rude, resentful when queried about a decision, and intrusive in matters of departmental administration with which a minister would not normally be engaged. He kept oral communication with his secretary to a minimum, preferring the exchange of written notes. Hasluck wrote exceptionally well but, since he was not always frank, his notes often failed to compensate for the want of candid discussion.

The mutually respectful, friendly and open relationship between Barwick and Tange seemed to me then, and still does now, the best possible example of a relationship between minister and secretary. It is the kind of relationship most likely to advance the government's and the minister's interests and most likely to be conducive to good governance. As secretary, I was fortunate to have such a relationship with both Alexander Downer and Tim Fischer.

Both ministers wanted, in addition to virtually daily contact with me, a regular weekly dialogue with the department's senior executive, in those weeks when they were not overseas. Mostly, I had separate meetings with the two ministers, but on occasion they would hold a joint meeting, including also the portfolio's two parliamentary secretaries. What both ministers sought from me and my colleagues were ideas, suggestions and robust debate about options. As secretary, I travelled mostly with the Prime Minister, but I also accompanied Alexander Downer on his first visit to South-East Asia and went to South Asia with Tim Fischer.

Fischer did not bring to the portfolio the inside knowledge of policy that Downer had, but he did bring a remarkable array of high-level friendships around Asia, developed as a result of his love of travel in the region, his prodigious memory for names, his personal warmth and his empathy with many Asian cultures. He also knew something of Latin America. As Deputy Prime Minister and Leader of the National Party, and as the devoted father of two young boys, he had exceptional demands on his time outside of his portfolio responsibilities.

Many observers took longer than they should have to appreciate that Fischer was shrewd and calculating, with an unusual ability — as he demonstrated to his cabinet colleagues and to other Trade ministers — to persuade others of his point of view (beware of Tim Fischer when he tells you that a situation is 'win-win'!). Fischer showed political courage and conviction in resisting his party on agricultural protection (and on gun ownership). He showed leadership — unquestionably controversial in the eyes of dedicated multilateralists — in his preference for bilateral approaches to international trade relations. He much preferred oral debate to long submissions and I was fortunate to have experienced trade deputies in Peter Grey and Joanna Hewitt,[5] both of whom excelled in extempore explanations of complex issues. Fischer was also exceptionally well served by Jenelle Bonnor on his staff.

While Fischer was Deputy Prime Minister, Downer was the senior portfolio minister and took the final decision on broad strategic directions, portfolio budget matters and diplomatic appointments. Downer had the advantage of having worked in the department as a diplomat for several years before pursuing his private sector and, then, political, career. He knew the department had a lot of talent and he knew what a well-directed department could accomplish.

In his first months as Foreign Minister, the media misjudged Downer. Many were convinced he would stumble. Even the conservative columnist Piers Akerman[6] forecast that before the year was out Downer would be posted to The Hague. Downer soon demonstrated to the media, however, that he was more than 'a dedicated Tory' (to use his term) and robust party politician. Those like me who had never worked with him previously found out quickly that he is passionately dedicated to advancing Australia's interests, highly intelligent, forthright, courageous, strategic and especially well read in history and economics. His knowledge in these areas had been as well concealed as Bill Hayden's knowledge of philosophy and art. Downer was particularly well served at that time by Greg Hunt [later to become a Parliamentary Secretary in the Howard government] and by Bill Farmer,[7] John Dauth[8] and the other deputy secretaries.

In some previous governments, the Department of Foreign Affairs and Trade had played second fiddle to the Department of Defence on broad strategic issues. In the Howard government, Downer dominated this area.

To lead a major Commonwealth department and be the minister's principal adviser on all important policy and strategic issues, a secretary has, in my view, five important tasks. He or she should:

- ensure that the Department has in place a set of well-understood goals and objectives;
- foster a collegial system for considering all current major policy issues and for anticipating future issues and opportunities;
- establish an appropriate pattern of delegation of responsibility, with accompanying accountability implications;
- make sure the Department has a well-understood management philosophy and an appropriate and effective allocation among divisions; and
- give high personal priority to staffing and human resource development policy.

Unquestionably, the major task for the secretary is running the department and inspiring departmental staff as they serve portfolio ministers. There are a host of other tasks: developing good relations with all parliamentarians concerned with foreign and trade policy and developing in particular a good working rapport with the relevant parliamentary committees; being accessible, subject to ministerial wishes, to the media, the business community and the academy; receiving foreign delegations; maintaining effective relations with the local diplomatic corps; and, last but not least, serving the Governor-General of the day by providing access to relevant information and, if required, material for use in speeches.

When I became secretary, the stated aim of the department, as set out in its Corporate Plan, was: 'To win a future for Australia in the world'. There is an element of idealism reflected in this aim, but also a streak of uncertainty and pessimism that was out of touch with the Howard Government's optimism and pragmatism. I changed this text to: 'To advance the interests of Australia and Australians internationally'.

The department's stated goals were also changed. The first goal became: 'To enhance Australia's security'. A previous goal, 'To advance Australia's standing as a good international citizen', was changed to: 'To strengthen global cooperation in ways which advance Australia's interests'. Highlighting Downer's strong commitment to give greater emphasis to consular issues, the goal of helping Australians overseas was changed to: 'To help Australian travellers and Australians overseas'. A new goal was added, reflected in the issuing of the 1997 *White Paper*: 'To promote public understanding of Australia's foreign and trade policy'. The framework of the Corporate Plan that I established in 1997 is, in terms of its stated aim and goals, still largely unchanged today.

A corporate plan as such has limited usefulness. However, the process of developing such a document and debating the relevant issues with senior and junior departmental staff is a valuable way of ensuring that the goals and objectives of a government are understood by the department as a whole.

I was fortunate as secretary to inherit the opening of the department's new building, which had been planned by the previous Government and, especially, by Gareth Evans. The opening by the Prime Minister was attended by four previous prime ministers: Sir John Gorton, Gough Whitlam, Malcolm Fraser and Bob Hawke. Two brilliant tapestries by the Victorian Tapestry Workshop were commissioned for display in the entrance foyer. The work, based on John Olsen's painting *Rising Suns over Australia Felix* reflects the building's confident nationalism. The other work, *Wamungu — My Mother's Country*, based on the painting of that title by Ginger Riley Munduwalawala, pays homage to indigenous culture.

The government had decided that the new building should be named the R.G. Casey Building, to honour Australia's then longest-serving foreign minister. Downer and Fischer readily agreed with my proposal that the selection of names for areas within the building should be made on a bipartisan basis and should also acknowledge the separate origins of the Department of Trade. Thus the department houses the H.V. Evatt Library, the Gareth Evans Theatrette and the J.D. Anthony Conference Room. There are meeting rooms named after former secretaries Sir John Crawford, William Hodgson, Atlee Hunt, Jim Scully, Sir Arthur Tange and Sir Alan Westerman. There is also the (Sir James) Plimsoll Dining Room. The street in front of the building is John McEwen Crescent, named in honour of Australia's longest-serving trade minister.

I felt it was important that, unlike the department's previous homes, this new building should convey a sense of Australia's history and remarkable artistic heritage. I commissioned a talented officer to assemble from the archives of the department, the National Library of Australia and major newspapers, a collection of photographs illustrating Australia's diplomatic history. Photographs from this collection are today a feature on virtually all of the Casey Building's walls. Antonia Syme, of Artbank, and my wife, Carole, helped ensure that original paintings by Australian artists are displayed in all significant rooms.

Given the demands associated with posting families overseas and with managing up to 90 overseas posts, the department has for a long time had in place a well-developed system of personnel administration. The dismantling of the old 'closed shop' culture of the department was begun by Sir Keith Waller and Mick Shann in the 1970s. The process was completed when Stuart Harris was secretary. During his term, when the former Department of Trade was amalgamated with the Department of Foreign Affairs in 1987, all systems were extensively reviewed and a conceptual framework for integrating foreign policy and trade policy issues was introduced.

Many outstanding people — including David Hay, Peter Henderson, David Goss, Frank Murray, Joanna Hewitt and a legion of others — have contributed to the well-deserved reputation for integrity and fairness enjoyed by DFAT's personnel system. In earlier years, the department had been slow to recruit women and even slower to promote them to senior levels. This situation had changed well before I became secretary. My contribution was to recommend more women for appointment as heads of mission than had ever previously been charged with this role.

More than one minister in the first Howard Government — but not Downer, Fischer or the Prime Minister — would cheerfully have outsourced diplomatic missions to the private sector if he felt this was feasible. No country of any significance (indeed, as far as I know, no country) has done this. The model of diplomatic missions managed by government has endured for hundreds of years, across cultures and countries, and has survived because it has been able to adapt effectively to dramatic changes in the international landscape and, in recent years, to profound changes in technology.

One very regrettable budgetary event during the first Howard Government concerned ownership of the Casey Building. The Minister of Finance was successful in persuading his colleagues — against the advice of Downer and Fischer — that the department's headquarters building should be sold to the Motor Trades Association of Australia. I remonstrated strongly with the Minister of Finance that this was an absurd proposal. It virtually guaranteed a private-sector owner access to monopoly rents after a grace period, since it was not practical for a foreign ministry to shop around for new locations, not least because of its communications installations. My representations were not successful.

Another complex issue brought on by budgetary pressures concerned journalists from the old Australian Information Service. They had joined the department, in most cases against their own wishes, as part of portfolio changes in 1987. My predecessor had sensibly started the process of reducing the number of journalists within the Department. I failed to see why, in the Internet age, the department needed 50 journalists to collate and distribute factual and positive information about Australia to the governments and media of other countries. One of the doyens of the Parliamentary Press Gallery, Wallace Brown, described as 'draconian and short-sighted' my view that there was more useful work the officers could do in the department or in the private sector. The majority of the Press Gallery evidently disagreed, since Brown's campaign failed and the decision was quickly accepted as sound public administration.

In 1997 I successfully negotiated a far-reaching Certified Agreement with the department's staff. This meant: major changes to salaries and the introduction of broad-banded salary classifications and salary packaging; a new system of performance pay and performance assessment; the elimination of centrally imposed restrictions on working hours, together with the old rules on increments and higher duties allowances; more streamlined procedures for dealing with inefficient or recalcitrant officers; and the introduction of formal arrangements for permanent part-time work, job sharing and home-based work.

In effect, these changes represented a first-time opportunity to gear employment conditions to the department's specific needs. In a secret ballot, the Agreement was approved by an overwhelming majority of staff. The changes were to bring less administration, enhanced organisational flexibility and a greater chance for staff to earn more through high performance. In addition, the department took over full responsibility for overseas allowances and conditions of service — issues that had been a continual source of frustration for over 50 years. This last set of changes was the culmination of a process to ensure that managers were responsible for the financial costs of their decisions.

The career paths of all of the Department's secretaries are remarkable for their diversity. Before I joined the Department, I studied economic statistics and mathematics at University and worked for three years for a major insurance company — studying to become an actuary.

I served six Coalition and three Labor governments. Successive Labor prime ministers appointed me as High Commissioner to Bangladesh, Ambassador to Indonesia and director-general of the Office of National Assessments. The present Government appointed me as secretary of DFAT. I had much earlier been appointed by the Coalition as Chief Executive for Special Trade Negotiations. It is one of the greatest privileges in Australia to be secretary of the Department of Foreign Affairs and Trade. For me it was the most professionally fulfilling role in 43 years of public service.

ENDNOTES

[1] Taylor, originally from Foreign Affairs, was First Assistant Secretary, International Division, Department of the Prime Minister and Cabinet.

[2] This statement was made in a speech entitled, 'Australia, Asia and the New Regionalism' that Keating gave at the Institute of Southeast Asian Studies in Singapore on 17 January 1996.

[3] Entitled *In the National Interest*, it was published in 1997.

[4] APEC is the Asian Pacific Economic Cooperation forum, set up in 1989 at the initiative of Australia and Japan under Bob Hawke's Prime Ministership.

[5] Joanna Hewitt was later appointed Secretary of the Department of Agriculture, Fisheries and Forestry (2004–07).

[6] Columnist for the News Limited Sydney newspaper, *The Daily Telegraph*.

[7] Bill Farmer was later appointed Secretary of the Department of Immigration and Multicultural Affairs (1998–2005).

[8] John Dauth was subsequently Australian Ambassador to the United Nations in New York (2001–06).

Epilogue: 'The job is never done'

John Butcher

In his prologue, Trevor Wilson observes that the period covered by the tenure of the five former DFAT secretaries encompassed times of 'intense and relentless public stress' for the department. During the years 1979–99, the application of 'new public management', with its emphases on performance, accountability and responsiveness, led to major transformations in the way Australian governments do business. The profound cultural changes wrought in the Australian Public Service (APS) over this period shaped the institutional and operational platform from which their successors, Dr Ashton Calvert (who served as secretary from 1998–2006) and Michael L'Estrange (the current DFAT secretary), would grapple with a volatile post-9/11 foreign and domestic policy environment defined, in part, by the 'War on Terror' (Bali, Iraq and David Hicks), failed or faltering regional states (East Timor, the Solomon Islands and Fiji) and global issues of the moment such as climate change (Kyoto and emissions trading), food security and energy security.

In response to a question put to him by a journalist at a 2 June 2008 press conference about rumoured 'policy paralysis' in the Department of Foreign Affairs and Trade, the Foreign Minister, the Hon. Stephen Smith, replied:

> [I]n a job like this, the job's never done. The work is never complete. The job is never done. And so I frankly don't pay much attention to what anonymous people might regard as a snapshot of a working day.
>
> The job is never done in this business. And in the end, the Australian people will make a judgement about whether the foreign policy that we adopted, and the public policy that we adopted, was ultimately for Australia's national interest.[1]

'The job is never done.' The minister's words have a truth and resonance with which both current and former secretaries of DFAT would surely agree. While the structural and systemic reforms of the Hawke-Keating and Howard governments surely transformed the operational culture and leadership style of the department, that transformation has on-going repercussions. If there is a truism about public administration, it is that stasis is illusory or, at best, temporary.

Ashton Calvert — punctilious professional and courageous thinker

In a media release on the occasion of the untimely death in November 2007 of former secretary Dr Ashton Calvert AC, then Minister for Foreign Affairs, Alexander Downer, remarked:

> Ashton Calvert's leadership of DFAT at a time of immense change and challenge in the international environment was his crowning achievement. Through his personal example and the standards he set, Ashton upheld clarity of focus and the highest standards of governance in the work of the department, while simultaneously delivering strong policy outcomes for Australia across a broad range of foreign policy and trade issues.[2]

Downer went on to say that Dr Calvert was 'frank and fearless in the best tradition of Australia's distinguished public service'. Downer's opinion was indeed shared by some on the other side of politics. The late Peter Cook, who was Trade Minister in the Keating government from 1993–94 and, later, professor at Curtin University, observed of Calvert before his death:

> Dr Calvert is a true foreign affairs professional. He is, as well, an exemplary public servant. You couldn't have served both the Keating Government as a Senior Advisor and the Howard Government as Secretary of the Department in positions of absolute trust unless you were anything short of being exemplary. In my experience Dr Calvert offers fearless advice and then conscientiously implements the decisions that are taken by the government. I think his own view is, which is both frightening and reassuring for ministers, is that ministers should get all the credit for what they do and they should get all the blame as well.[3]

Paul Keating's biographer, Don Watson, described Aston Calvert as 'an astute, punctilious professional of undisguised ambition and a streak of zeal' who, as advisor on international affairs, had earned Keating's respect as 'a good and courageous thinker' (Watson 2002: 71; 406). Keating himself said of Calvert that he was 'an outstanding diplomat' with a 'hard-headed, take-no-prisoner approach to international affairs'.[4]

It is ironic, therefore, that Graeme Dobell[5], in a 2003 critique of what he termed a culture of 'diplomatic compliance' in DFAT on Calvert's watch, asserted:

> … self-censorship has become an ambassadorial art form; well-understood protocols ensure ministers are not told what they don't want to hear and professional discipline is reinforced by a 'culture of compliance'. (Dobell 2003: 67)

Dobell's article laments the impact on the 'ethos of DFAT' of the 'series of revolutions imposed on the public service by the Hawke-Keating and Howard governments' aimed at transforming its management culture (Dobell 2003: 69). Of course, Dobell is not alone in his fears that the capacity to offer considered and impartial policy advice has been compromised by a heightened emphasis on 'responsiveness' to government. Here it should be noted that the principle of 'responsiveness' is enshrined in the APS Values in the *Public Service Act* 1999 in the following terms:

> the APS is responsive to the Government in providing frank, honest, comprehensive, accurate and timely advice and in implementing the Government's policies and programs (S9, Part 3, 10(f)).

The concern, as expressed by Dobell, seems to be that 'responsiveness', in the case of DFAT, has tipped into political compliance and, even, complicity.

Such concerns are not exclusive to DFAT. A number of commentators hold that the qualities of 'frank and fearless' have long been in decline across the APS. Indeed, in a recent ANZSOG monograph, *Whatever Happened to Frank and Fearless? The impact of new public management on the Australian Public Service*, Kathy MacDermott clinically examines the evidence for such a decline and comes to similar conclusions. It is not, however, my purpose here to digress into a critique of the evolving relationship between the administrative and executive arms of government in Australia — others have done that capably and at length elsewhere. Instead, I wish to briefly explore from the perspective of the players themselves, the principal operational (as opposed to policy) challenges facing DFAT in the contemporary era.

Calvert himself — perhaps owing to the 'clarity and focus' of which Downer spoke — well understood the practical operational challenges faced by a department like DFAT. Dobell, citing Calvert, portrayed the 'realpolitik' within which departmental secretaries now work:

> The man at the centre of DFAT, the secretary, Ashton Calvert, argues there was never a public service golden age: 'The implication seems to be that there was some previous period when public servants were free to decide things themselves, which is not what I recall. I don't think it would be healthy or democratic if that were the case.' He agrees there has been cultural change but sees it more as a response to staff cuts, technological change and the complexity of issues modern government confronts. Foreign Affairs must be more of a team player in a whole-of-government process: 'We most certainly are much better integrated and better embedded in the broader public service than before'. (Dobell 2003: 72-73)

Of course, Calvert, at different points in his career, walked both sides of the fence, first as a foreign policy adviser to former Prime Minister Paul Keating and then as a bureaucrat. In some respects, the shift from political insider to government official might have seemed to him rather constraining. In his book, *Engagement: Australia Faces the Asia-Pacific*, Keating (2000) draws a clear distinction between the *modus operandi* of a policy adviser and a departmental secretary:

> Next to the foreign minister, the adviser's job is, I believe, the second most important in the Australian foreign policy firmament. *Free of the administrative burden which the secretaryship of the Department of Foreign Affairs and Trade has*, the adviser's job is principally about policy. But unlike most policy jobs, *it carries with it the live conduit of power.* (emphasis added)[6]

The transition from the role of policy advisor to departmental secretary might have been a difficult one, both for Calvert and the man who succeeded him, Michael L'Estrange, owing to the 'administrative burden' of which Keating speaks. Not only is the secretary expected to advise the minister and the government in relation to a complex and dynamic policy frontier, he/she is required to offer clear executive leadership and governance oversight in a department with over 3000 staff (including almost 1500 staff recruited overseas); a budget appropriation of over $832 million; and non-financial assets valued at over $1.5 billion.[7] In addition, the department contains seven portfolio agencies and administers 38 principal Acts. If secretaries are accorded less freedom to wander the policy landscape, it is because their responsibilities are larger and more diverse while their accountabilities are more pointed. While the popular perception of the secretary's role may have been shaped by *'Yes Minister'* caricatures of British Permanent secretaries effectively running their own foreign policy agendas in parallel to those of the government, such is not — and has, perhaps, never been — the case in Australia. More to the point, senior executives' 'accountability for performance' has certainly been heightened over the course of the last 25 years of public sector reform.

In a 1999 speech on 'The role of DFAT at the turn of the Century', Calvert observed that economic globalisation played a part in transforming the way DFAT does its work:

> The Australian economy is now more open, internationally oriented and competitive than ever before.

> As a consequence, more and more Australian companies of various sizes are increasingly engaged in international trade in an increasing number of foreign markets in an ever-widening range of products and services.

> This means, of course, a bigger, not a smaller, role for DFAT in helping these companies by negotiating improved market access for Australian products and services either through the WTO or bilaterally, and by working with other governments to streamline procedures, harmonise standards and better manage quarantine arrangements.[8]

In addition, he noted that advances in information technology had 'produced a totally new dynamic in the international dissemination of policy-relevant information and proposals' with the result 'that many processes of bilateral and multilateral negotiations that were hitherto handled quietly by governments behind closed doors are now subject to virtually immediate scrutiny by informed groups in relevant countries'. He added that '[t]hese developments are certainly not something that DFAT resists' and drew attention to his department's efforts to make its website 'attractive and useful to the general public'. He also acknowledged that, in keeping with the main currents of contemporary public sector management, the '[d]isciplines of transparency, accountability and policy contestability are very healthy for an organisation like DFAT'.

With respect to the operational and budgetary challenges faced by the department under his stewardship, he observed that much of the Department's management reform work had been:

> ... concentrated on finding savings, for example, through judicious thinning of our overseas positions, including through replacement by locally employed staff.
>
> At home, we have targeted our internal administrative practices, delivering important savings through streamlining and some outsourcing.
>
> We have been able to use to real advantage the new flexibility available to departments under the Government's public-service reforms.
>
> We now have the ability to set our own conditions, for example in relation to overseas terms and conditions for our staff.
>
> Another area of opportunity has been the freedom that agencies now have in agreement-making to set the pay and other employment conditions for all staff.[9]

Calvert remarked that DFAT, in 1999, was 'clearly different from the former Department of Foreign Affairs before its amalgamation with the Department of Trade in 1987' and drew attention to 'the new emphasis that is now given to delivering practical services to a range of Australian clients beyond the Government itself' as well as to 'meeting the policy challenges we face in a modern, dynamic and effective way'.

In a June 2001 speech at a ceremony to launch the DFAT display in Canberra for the centenary of the Australian Public Service, he alluded to the stereotypes of the foreign service portrayed in the media and drew attention to what he considered 'the acid test for the department':

> That is, the work that we do providing passports for Australians to travel overseas and helping Australians who run into problems abroad. To put this in perspective, in 1999–2000 3.3 million Australians travelled abroad. Over the same period, we issued almost 1.15 million passports. That's one every 27 seconds. Each year DFAT assists more than 20,000 Australians in serious difficulty through our consular network of more than 150 points of service throughout the world. And over the past three years alone, DFAT staff in Canberra and on the ground have coordinated major efforts to ensure the safety of Australians affected by civil unrest in Indonesia and East Timor, Fiji, the Solomons and Papua New Guinea.[10]

In 2003, Calvert again reflected on the structural reforms pursued by DFAT that rendered it capable of being 'nimble and versatile, while still able to nurture and deploy a broad array of expertise and professional skills'.

> Our goal has been to have not just high-quality and highly motivated staff, but staff who are well led and well managed; and staff who can deliver outcomes with respect to the Government's policy objectives and have careers that are professionally and personally fulfilling.[11]

Calvert remarked that 'DFAT, like all public-sector agencies, has embraced very significant change over the past few years in response to the imperative for smaller, more cost-effective government' and outlined a number of structural reform initiatives aimed at strengthening the organisation, including:

- centralising the management of staffing (while at the same time maintaining DFAT's 'traditionally decentralised flows of policy advice to ministers') in order to confer an increased capacity to be 'responsive, flexible and efficient with respect to the deployment of staff' whilst ensuring fairness and transparency in relation to postings, placements and promotions;
- decreasing the number of staff working in the corporate management and corporate service areas 'in a rational and efficient manner, without detracting from [DFAT's] pursuit of the Government's other key policy objectives'; and
- delivering savings with respect to internal administrative practices through streamlining and outsourcing and leveraging technology.

He remarked that these changes enabled 'a much sharper focus on the Department's core foreign and trade policy responsibilities, and on the practical services we provide to the Australian public.'

Michael L'Estrange — Secretary via 'the road less travelled'

In his six-and-a-half years as secretary, Ashton Calvert shepherded important and extensive reforms credited 'sharpening the Department's focus and lifting its morale and productivity'.[12] These important legacies were appreciated by his successor, Michael L'Estrange who, in 2005, was able to observe: 'I inherited a department that worked extremely well' (Malone 2006: 37). Nevertheless, he added that the job 'is relentless and unpredictable to an extent because you are reacting to events' (Malone 2006: 39).

In a 2006 address to the National Press Club entitled 'Responding to Twenty-First Century Challenges: DFAT in a Changing World', L'Estrange noted the practical challenges faced by an organisation as complex as DFAT in which:

- Australia-based staff number just over 2000, of whom around a quarter are posted overseas at any one time;
- overseas postings include 87 Embassies, High Commissions, Consulates and Multilateral Missions in 74 States; and
- operations are conducted in 61 different currencies.

He also drew attention to the growing demand for consular services and support for travellers and Australian's abroad, including:

- substantial consular support services to Australians overseas (just under 16,000 cases in the year to June 2006);
- regular updates to travel advisories to 152 destinations; and
- issuing over 1.2 million passports to eligible Australians (in 2005–06).[13]

L'Estrange reflected on the fact that the APS and DFAT had changed fundamentally in the 25 years since he joined the public service, as a result of management reforms and broader environmental changes resulting in DFAT being 'intricately involved in the wide-ranging policy implications of increasing globalisation and because across so many areas of national policy — from security issues to national economic competitiveness to many others — the interaction between domestic and international considerations is more active and porous than ever before'.[14]

In a 2006 article published in *The Sydney Papers,* L'Estrange refers to the 'whole of government' realities of contemporary governance, noting that the time was 'long gone' when 'matters to do with "foreign policy" were clearly demarcated from those relating to "domestic policy"' (L'Estrange 2006: 74). He goes on to say that, more than ever before, 'Australia's international and domestic interests are significantly more aligned today — whether it be in relation to security issues or economic growth or national competitiveness' (L'Estrange 2006: 74-75). Mindful of 'whole-of-government realities', L'Estrange observes the priority attached to 'developing close and effective' relationships with 'the many departments and agencies which have important international operations or comparative benchmarks that increasingly share areas of intersection' (L'Estrange 2006: 74-75).

According to L'Estrange, the position of secretary has provided 'unique insights into the scale of the difficulties, dangers and personal risks that officers of the Department can face' in the course of their duties. His summary of the qualities and attributes required of DFAT officers can be seen as a microcosm of the challenges facing the department as a whole:

> ... we require of those who work today for the Department of Foreign Affairs and Trade a wide range of attributes. We require of them diplomatic skills — not of an effete, outdated or arcane kind but of a practical, hard-nosed and outcomes-oriented character. We require informed judgment and carefully focused activism. We require of our officers high quality advocacy skills to be applied within and beyond government. We require of them an awareness of appropriate opportunities for Australian export enterprises and a capacity to support them. And we require of them personal qualities that enable them to support and assist Australians in times of emergency or tragic loss, and to cope themselves with the pressures that they and their families come under in particular parts of the world. (L'Estrange 2006: 75)

L'Estrange continues the tradition of scholar turned mandarin — although, 'mandarin' may not be the most appropriate term, for as was observed in a 1997 article in the *Sydney Morning Herald*, men like L'Estrange 'represent "Washminster" — the combination of old-style Westminster governance where public servants operate at arm's length from the elected politicians, and Washington's system where all senior jobs are political appointments, spilled when the presidency changes hands' (Brough and Millett, 1997). Although he says of his career trajectory 'I came to the position of Secretary by a "road less travelled" compared to the career path of my predecessors'[15], like Calvert, he was a Rhodes Scholar and studied at Oxford University, earning a First Class Honours in philosophy, politics and economics (Calvert also gained a Doctorate from Oxford University, in mathematics).[16]

Like Calvert too, L'Estrange has had to navigate some tricky political territory. Calvert had worked closely with Keating as a senior advisor on international affairs, yet his professionalism allowed him to rise above any perceived political association to be appointed secretary of DFAT by John Howard. In a similar way, L'Estrange continues as secretary under the Rudd government despite a reputation 'as a Liberal Party insider and conservative intellectual' as well as 'a close political ally and confidant' of former Prime Minister, John Howard (Malone 2006: 40). Clearly, professionalism and intellectual rigour are highly prized in this post as is experience in senior diplomatic posts (L'Estrange was High Commissioner to the United Kingdom from 2000 to 2005; Calvert was Ambassador to Japan from 1993 to 1998).

Still, the transition has not been entirely smooth sailing. In a recent article in the *Sunday Mail* veteran journalist, Glen Milne, alleged that L'Estrange had been deliberately omitted from the Prime Minister's entourage on his recent foray overseas, missing key meetings with US President George W. Bush, members of the US Congress and the US Chamber of Commerce, presumably because of his reputation as a 'Howard loyalist' (Milne 2008).[17] Indeed, it is possible that working with a Prime Minister who is himself a former career diplomat might be a greater source of potential tension than any ideological differences, real or imagined. In any case, a degree of initial wariness is in keeping with the expected 'rough and tumble' of a period of political and administrative transition in which new governments generally hold suspect the impartiality and capacity of the bureaucracy, preferring the counsel of ministerial advisers, favoured lobbyists and assorted apparatchiks. Transition-of-government is a period of relationship-building and trust-building. The Rudd government's transition to office has, in fact, been remarkably smooth in marked contrast to the purge of departmental heads that followed Howard's ascension in 1996.

The future

Certainly, a transition of government would form a part of the fabric of the broader challenge of 'discerning clearly the elements of continuity and change in the international environment' to which L'Estrange addressed himself in his 2006 article. In the article he observes that, while not a new challenge for the department, it is nevertheless a challenge that 'bears very directly on the role and responsibilities of the Department of Foreign Affairs and Trade' because, 'in its modern form, it is a more complex, demanding and variable one than it has ever been':

> Meeting this challenge requires the Department to show innovation and flexibility in responding to the dynamics of positive change. But it also calls for consistency, realism and steadiness of purpose in responding to the dynamics of continuity where the requirements for security and stability have not changed and where Australian interests are enduring.
>
> That is why issues of change and continuity lie at the heart of the Department's responsibilities and why they are so critical to the advancement of Australian interests. (L'Estrange 2006: 83)

In a sense, the administrative, management and leadership challenges faced by Calvert and L'Estrange (and any future secretary of the department) reflect the continuation of about 25 years of ongoing and intensive structural reform and organisational change. Indeed, each of the secretaries whose experience is shared in this volume has had to constructively manage significant structural and institutional changes. The last 25 years has also seen significant domestic social and political transformation, international and geopolitical realignment and economic repositioning. So too, the period has been characterised by rapid and profound technological change — not least of which is the revolution in communications technologies that have dramatically transformed the way large organisations do business. If the challenges, as observed by L'Estrange, are 'complex, demanding and variable', it is because the drivers of foreign and trade policy — not to mention institutional, structural and micro-economic reform — are similarly complex, demanding and variable. Change, and the need to respond positively and creatively to change, never stops.

Which, of course, is just another way of saying 'the job is never done'.

References

Dobell, Graeme 2002, 'Diplomatic Compliance'. *Griffith Review*, Spring 2003, pp. 65-79.

Keating, Paul 2000, *Engagement: Australia Faces the Asia-Pacific*, Macmillan, 2000.

Koutsoukis, Jason 2008, 'Thanks for the Enemies', *The Age*. March 16, 2008, accessed 26 June 2008 at http://www.theage.com.au/articles/2008/03/15/1205472160373.html

L'Estrange, Michael 2006, 'Continuity and Change in the Pursuit of Australia's International Interests [online]', *Sydney Papers, The*; Volume 18, Issue 3/4; Winter/Spring 2006; 72-83, availability: <http://search.informit.com.au/documentSummary;dn=412253896300840; res=E-LIBRARY> ISSN: 1035-7068 [cited 24 Jun 2008].

MacDermott, Kathy 2008, *Whatever Happened to Frank and Fearless: The impact of new public management on the Australian Public Service*, ANZSOG Monograph Series, ANU E Press, http://epress.anu.edu.au/frank_fearless_citation.html

Malone, Paul 2006, *Australian Department Heads Under Howard*, ANZSOG Monograph Series, ANU E Press, http://epress.anu.edu.au/dept_heads_citation.html

Milne, Glen 2008, 'Rudd left key aide off flight', *Sunday Mail*, 20 June 2008, accessed 24 June at http://www.news.com.au/adelaidenow/story/ 0,22606,23901950-5006301,00.html

Brough, Jodie and Michael Millett 1997, 'The Axemen Cometh', *Sydney Morning Herald*, November 1, 1997, accessed 24 June 2008, at http://australianpolitics.com/executive/howard/pre-2002/axemen-cometh.shtml

Watson, Don 2002, *Recollections of a Bleeding Heart — A portrait of Paul Keating*, Random House.

ENDNOTES

[1] Source: The Hon Stephen Smith MP, Australian Minister for Foreign Affairs, Press Conference, 2 June 2008. http://www.foreignminister.gov.au/transcripts/2008/080602_pc.html

[2] Source: The Hon. Alexander Downer, MP, Media Release, 16 November 2007. 'Dr Ashton Calvert AC'. http://www.foreignminister.gov.au/releases/2007/fa142_07.html

[3] Source: 'A confident and distinctive foreign policy', Speech given by Dr Ashton Calvert on the occasion of the seventh JCPML Anniversary Lecture marking the 60th anniversary of John Curtin's death, 5 July 2005. http://john.curtin.edu.au/events/speeches/calvert.html

[4] Source: Paul Keating, *Engagement*, http://www.keating.org.au/engagement.cfm

[5] Dobell is the Foreign Affairs and Defence Correspondent for Australian Broadcasting Corporation's *Radio Australia* and is a close observer of Australian political affairs.

[6] Source: Paul Keating, *Engagement*, http://www.keating.org.au/engagement.cfm

[7] Department of Foreign Affairs and Trade, *Annual Report 2005-2006*. http://www.dfat.gov.au/dept/annual_reports/05_06/index.html

[8] Source: 'The Role of DFAT at the Turn of the Century', Address to the Canberra Branch of the Australian Institute Of International Affairs by Dr Ashton Calvert, Secretary, DFAT, Canberra, 4 February 1999. http://www.dfat.gov.au/media/speeches/department/990201_dfats_role.html

[9] Source: 'The Role of DFAT at the Turn of the Century', Address to the Canberra Branch of the Australian Institute Of International Affairs by Dr Ashton Calvert, Secretary, DFAT, Canberra, 4 February 1999. http://www.dfat.gov.au/media/speeches/department/990201_dfats_role.html

[10] Source: 'APS Centenary', speech by Dr Ashton Calvert, Secretary, DFAT, at a ceremony to launch the DFAT centenary display, Canberra, 19 June 2001.

http://www.dfat.gov.au/media/speeches/department/0106_centaps.html

[11] Source: 'The Role of DFAT at the Turn of the Century', Address to the Canberra Branch of the Australian Institute Of International Affairs by Dr Ashton Calvert, Secretary, DFAT, Canberra, 4 February 1999. http://www.dfat.gov.au/media/speeches/department/990201_dfats_role.html

[12] Source: Brief biography of Dr Ashton Calvert, John Curtin Prime Ministerial Library, Curtin University of Technology. http://john.curtin.edu.au/events/speeches/calvertbiog.html

[13] Source: Michael L'Estrange, Secretary, Department of Foreign Affairs and Trade, 'Responding to Twenty-First Century Challenges: DFAT in a Changing World', Address to the National Press Club, Canberra, 27 September 2006. http://www.dfat.gov.au/media/speeches/department/060927_npc.html

[14] Ibid.

[15] Source: Michael L'Estrange, Secretary - Department of Foreign Affairs and Trade. Speech: Continuity and Change in the Pursuit of Australia's International Interests. 6 July 2006. http://www.dfat.gov.au/media/speeches/department/060706_international_interests.html

[16] Sources: Department of Foreign Affairs and Trade, Biographical Details for Mr. Michael L'Estrange, AO, Secretary - Department of Foreign Affairs and Trade.
http://www.dfat.gov.au/dept/exec/lestrange_bio.html; Business Week Executive Profile of Ashton Calvert AC. http://investing.businessweek.com/businessweek/research/stocks/people/person.asp?personId=20460755&capId=862503&previousCapId=631759&previousTitle=Lonza%20Group%20AG

[17] Of course, the fact that L'Estrange remains secretary of DFAT at all baffled some observers. In a recent article in *The Age*, Jodie Brough and Michael Millett observed that 'although you couldn't fit a cigarette paper between Howard and L'Estrange over the past 20 years, the Rudd Government has embraced him'. L'Estranger than fiction, perhaps?

Appendix 1: Data on DFAT staff numbers and budget allocations

for the financial years 1979–80, 1984–85, 1989–90, 1994–95 and 1999–2000

DFAT STAFF NUMBERS	1979 (calendar)	1980 (calendar)	1984–85 (financial)	1989–90 (financial)	1994–95 (financial)	1999–2000 (financial)
Total Australia-based staff	2,373	2,341	2,251	2,677	2,600	2,603
Locally engaged staff	2,128	2,158	1,972	2,009	1,603	1,580
Total DFAT staff	4,501	4,499	4223[2]	4,686[2]	4,203	4,183
	(31 Dec 1979)	(31 Dec 1980)	(30 June 1985)	(30 June 1990)	(30 June 1995)	(30 June 2000)

DFAT ANNUAL EXPENDITURE	1979–80 (financial year)	1984–85 (financial year)	1989–90 (financial year)	1994–95 (financial year)	1999–2000 (financial year)
Total DFAT outlays	$619,045,000	$1,208,359,000	$1,458,801,384	$1,623,522,131	$1,867,258,000
DFAT expenditure as per centage of total Australian Government payments	1.99%	1.89%	1.64%	1.32%	1.22%
Australian Government Payments[1]	$31.041 m	$63.639 m	$88.882 m	$122.901 m	$153.030 m
	(30 June 1980)	(30 June 1985)	(30 June 1990)	(30 June 1995)	(30 June 2000)

[1] Australian Government general government sector payments
[2] Total (Foreign Affairs excluding ADAB (1984/1985) / AIDAB (1989/1990))
Sources: DFAT Annual Reports for 1979–80, 1984–85, 1989–90, 1994–95 and 1999–2000.

www.ingramcontent.com/pod-product-compliance
Lightning Source LLC
Chambersburg PA
CBHW041141170426
43200CB00022B/2990